TRAIL MIX

STORIES OF

YOUTH OVERCOMING

ADVERSITY

DANIELLE CORRIVEAU

FOREWORD BY PICABO STREET

AFTERWORD BY DORI BIESTER

PHOTOGRAPHS BY
JOHN CORRIVEAU, JOHN FIELDER, PADGETT MCFEELY

Corvo Communications

ISBN: 0-9702366-0-3

Cover and book design: Gretchen Ray, TM Design, Denver, Colorado
Photography / Artwork:
John Corriveau, Grand Rapids, Michigan – Pages 24, 49, 57, 63, 69, 75, 81, 89, and 101
Rene Atchinson, Sagebrush Productions, Littleton, Colorado – Author, Pages 11 and 33
John Fielder, Westcliffe Publishing, Englewood, Colorado
Padgett McFeely, Denver, Colorado

Library of Congress Card Number: 00-111995

This book is dedicated to two very special people:
my father and my friend

Peter Corriveau,
who is a great golf competitor and an incredible father.
I am grateful for your endless unconditional support. I also am grateful
you taught me how to keep my head down and swing through the ball.
That direction led to so many wonderful matches with you on courses
near and far from home. May there be many, many more!

Jennifer Parrott,
who shared countless cups of coffee with me while helping to
define the direction of this work. I cherish you as my friend and
admire you even more.

Thank you to

The parents and children who bravely shared their stories, strength, and hope with me — including those in this book and others who gave their time to tell me their stories.

Picabo Street for carving time out of her busy schedule to contribute the Foreword. She is a vivacious young woman, committed to helping youth and spreading the word about brain injury prevention. It has been a privilege and a joy to work with her.

John Fielder for quickly responding to my letter. I am touched by your generosity.

Padgett McFeely for agreeing to include your beautiful artwork.

Dad and Mom for your encouragement.

John Corriveau for being an outstanding photographer and an even better brother.

Gretchen Ray for using your gift of creativity to design the pages of this book. You are a great friend and a beautiful bride. I am honored to stand up for you.

Janis Leibs Dworkis for thorough and thoughtful editing. I appreciated every highlight from you.

Kate Kelly for being at the same address in Maryland. I am so glad I found you again and that you agreed to give your expertise to this work.

Dianne Gum for your insight and enthusiasm for writing. Thank you for the guidance.

Jackie Waldman for being my beacon. I am so thankful that I fielded a phone call that made all the difference in the world to this project.

Mary Saracino for being a wonderful author and friend. Thanks, Peanut. You are an inspiration.

Brian Carpenter for lending your legal expertise. Thanks, Counselor.

Vince Doerr and Hunter for sharing the trails with me and listening to the latest "book" story.

Michael Durkin, Kelley Cahill, Richard Audsley, and **Laura Rogers** for giving me the opportunity to work for Mile High United Way.

Faithful friends for providing much needed support, welcome distractions, and comic relief.

God for compassionately listening to my childlike prayers.

ABOUT THE ARTISTS

JOHN CORRIVEAU

John Corriveau, who has been an editorial/commercial photographer for more than two decades, has spent the last seven years working in Grand Rapids, Michigan. He currently runs an independent business with a client list that includes Steelcase Inc., Herman Miller, Calvin College, Grand Valley State University, J.W. Messner Inc., and Ameritech.

Corriveau is a regular contributor to *Grand Rapids Magazine* and *Grand Rapids Parent Magazine.* Additional publishing credits include the *New York Times, Le Monde, U.S. News & World Report, Time, Newsweek, Ebony, Symphony,* and *World Trade.* Corriveau also has received commissions from the Smithsonian Institution and the Public Museum of Grand Rapids, where his work is on permanent display.

JOHN FIELDER

John Fielder is a nationally renowned nature photographer, publisher, teacher, and preservationist. He is the photographer of 30 exhibit-format books and guidebooks, most about his home state of Colorado. Fielder has worked tirelessly to promote the protection of Colorado's open space and wildlands. His photography has influenced people and legislation, earning him recognition from many conservation groups, including the Sierra Club's Ansel Adams Award. His most recent books include the best-selling *Colorado: 1870–2000* and *A Colorado Winter.* He lives with his family in Greenwood Village, Colorado.

PADGETT MCFEELY

Padgett McFeely began cultivating an interest in photography at Orange Coast College in California. To create the fantastic imagery and surreal edge characteristic of her work, McFeely hand paints each of her black-and-white photographic prints. She uses oil, but also includes watercolor dye, pencil, pastel, or crayon. She applies paint primarily using cotton and cotton swabs. She is now experimenting with heavy paint application.

McFeely holds numerous awards of recognition for her artwork, including first place in photography in the Vail Arts Festival, and has been published in the Best of Photography in *Photographer's Forum Magazine.* Her work is in private collections in England, New York, Hawaii, San Diego, San Francisco, Washington, D.C., Chicago, Denver, Los Angeles, Michigan, Arizona, and Puerto Rico. She now lives in Denver, Colorado.

REFLECTIONS ON NATURE

John Fielder
Nature Photographer
Greenwood Village, Colorado

Rocky Mountain National Park became a park in 1915 because of the thoughtful photography and insightful writing of Enos Mills. He was an outspoken advocate for protecting a 400 square-mile place that was being lost to development. These are some of the eloquent words he used to accomplish his mission in life, composed more than 100 years ago:

> *"Parks are first aid — also prevention. They prevent more law-breaking than policeman; cure more than physicians; give more ideas than sermons; more development than schools. The pace and pressure of modern life, its daily duties and examinations, require that everyone must be steadily refreshed, and for this sustaining and ever-invoking refreshment nature is a perennial, cheering source.*
>
> *Nature takes mind and body, and puts them at their best. Here one comes to know himself or herself, and to be the self he or she would like to be. Nature is the lifesaver of the race; the great out-of-doors is the lifesaving station of the nation. Probably the best way to delay death, the best medicine to lengthen life, is to take to the woods. This life-sustaining prescription is most effective as a preventive, and should be regularly used. Like a sermon, it should be taken once in a while whether needed or not! It is Mother Nature's cure-all, and there are no substitutes just as good."*

I know what Enos Mills knew. When we reinforce and renew our relationship with all things natural and wild, we thrive both physically and mentally.

Personally, I do not even need to be in the woods to feel healthier. Just knowing that such places exist makes me feel better. The mere knowledge that there is a place to retreat from the pressures of society and modern life, is psychological salve, and may ultimately be physiological salve. My relationship with nature, with the more permanent things in life, give me the strength and confidence to overcome all obstacles put in my way. I hope that your relationship with nature allows the same.

— *John Fielder*

TABLE OF CONTENTS

AT THE TRAILHEAD

I nearly missed the opportunity to create this book. Driving frantically,
through an unfamiliar Denver neighborhood, I contemplated giving up
finding the writing seminar that I had enrolled in months earlier.
Arriving late, breathless, and unprepared, I departed, six hours later,
inspired, determined and focused on producing this work.

I darted into the room and landed on the one remaining folding chair. The participants were already taking turns talking about their "potential books." They had questions about agents, editors, and publishers. They related their struggles with particular points in their manuscripts. I, on the other hand, didn't have a thought about a book I was going to write. So for the next six hours I listened.

I listened to my classmates share about their personal histories in relation to their books, which led me to think about changes I had recently made in my own life. I had moved to Colorado to escape the hustle of Washington, D.C. Like many, the beauty of the mountains lured me to live closer to them. I had also taken a job with Mile High United Way, where I learned about people who had experienced miraculous changes in their lives after receiving support, encouragement, and acknowledgement from the organization's agencies.

The instructor disrupted my reverie when she directed each student to write about his or her book. When she addressed me, she blurted out, "You write about...whatever."

In a fury of writing, my blank page became a mess of scribbled, rough ideas, blending my thoughts of the day. During the last thirty minutes of class, my vision for the book became clear. I was filled with a driving desire to put into writing stories that could bring hope and to gift-wrap those stories with colorful images of nature.

That week, I made a list of organizations that might have wilderness programs for children. I knew about a program called Camp Comfort, a grief camp for kids, offered by Mount Evans Home Care and Hospice in Evergreen, Colorado, through my work with United Way.

And that is how I met John Taylor.

John's father had died suddenly. When that happened, John had closed down emotionally — until he went to Camp Comfort.

During the interview at John's house, he shared the story of life before his father's death. And life after his father was gone. He squirmed on the floor in front of the fireplace, talking in the direction of his socks, while the red light on my tiny tape recorder, placed on the coffee table in front of him, glowed. I leaned forward from the overstuffed white sofa and slowly asked him, "Tell me more."

Finally we moved on to questions about camp. The atmosphere took a dramatic turn. John sat up on his knees and leaned on the coffee table. His tone, previously somber, turned to confident. He spoke about outdoor camp activities — fishing, hiking, swimming, canoeing. He talked about the craft projects, memory books, the circle discussions and about the relief he felt when he was able to talk with other kids about losing his father.

That evening, after that interview, I really understood the tremendous effect Camp Comfort had on John and his mother, Jamie.

Two years, and many memories, later here is *Trail Mix*.

All of the young people in this book discovered something about themselves through their experiences at camp. They experienced it through nature. Nature sets an incredible stage for discovery. Her theater offers high ceilings and ample room to run. They found it through the camaraderie of their peers. They uncovered it through the support of adults — the professionals, parents, and volunteers — who opened the door for these youth, guiding, but not dictating, their discoveries.

Each of their stories relays a graceful strength in confronting challenges, whether those formidable obstacles include rock climbing, overcoming painful memories, or staring down illnesses.

The children and families, through their words, have reaffirmed for me that, in spite of great adversity, hope is always within reach. They've changed my life because they have given me inspiration I can draw from when I feel defeated. I invite you to get to know them too.

When the walls of the city seem unbearably close, and the sterility of e-mailing and instant messaging become overwhelming, I encourage you to immerse yourself in the images in this book, until you can traverse that ground for real. It is also my hope that you may listen with your heart, hear the extraordinary messages these young adults share, and allow their triumphs to lift your spirits.

I sincerely thank those who contribute their time, energy, enthusiasm, creativity and financial resources to the wilderness programs that have helped these young people and their families. That support makes it possible to teach children that perceived limitations can be conquered.

—*Danielle Corriveau*

Photograph © John Fielder 2001

FOREWORD

Picabo Street
1998 Olympic Gold Medalist
Super Giant Slalom
Nagano, Japan

I started skiing at age five, and at age ten, I started dreaming about skiing in the Olympics. Through years of practice, victories, bumps, and bruises, I kept moving in the direction of my dream.

When I was thirteen, I qualified for the Junior Olympics in Alaska. I went, and I won all the races. That was the beginning of my Olympic experience. I realized my dream in 1994 when I won a silver medal. After that I won nine World Cup downhill victories in 1995 and 1996 and a world championship in 1996.

I love skiing and the freedom it gives me. When I am skiing downhill, negotiating the mountain, riding through the powder, everything, but that moment, leaves me. I know when I am on skis that that is exactly where I am meant to be. It's my essence. Yet I have faced some frightening situations on the slopes. The scariest was the brain injury I suffered in Sweden, just days before the 1998 Olympic games in Nagano, Japan.

It was the World Cup, and I started the race totally confident that I was going to win. I truly believed I would be going to Nagano with a win under my belt.

I was skiing the race hard. I was charging, totally attacking the run. Then WHAM! My ski prereleased. Within seconds, I was on only one ski, completely off-balance and out of control. My mind instantly focused on survival as I tried to get back in control and out of crash mode.

I flew up and over my ski. The side of my face smacked on the ground as I rolled, rolled, rolled. Through all of this I was still trying to think of how to stop the crash! I was working hard to get my head off the ground, but my body kept moving down the hill. I knew the fence was somewhere close. Too close.

My face slammed into the fence.

I sat up slowly, dazed. My goggles felt like they were digging into my brow. When I pushed them onto my forehead, everything went black and I passed out. A few seconds later, I woke up to the French team's coach wiping snow off my face. My whole body was tingly. I was confused about what happened.

The coaches helped me up, but I buckled immediately. Everything was blurry. I couldn't focus on anything from the horizon down, and that scared me. My eyes glazed over. At the bottom of the hill they loaded me into a helicopter and flew me to the hospital.

After looking at the CAT scan, the doctors knew I had a brain injury. It was less than two weeks before the Olympics.

The doctors and coaches questioned whether I could go. They watched me, and tested me constantly. I knew they were evaluating, but to me, there was no question. The only thing that mattered was being able to hold my head up in my tuck while I was skiing downhill. I decided if I could do that, I was going. I became more focused than I had ever been in my life.

Once again, I was in survival mode.

I thought to myself, "I have to channel this. I have to save this energy for the race. I have to use my frustration to help me in the race." I turned that frustration into pure, clean power.

I adopted the mentality of the well-known football coach Vince Lombardi, "Adversity makes heroes." Saying that to myself amped me up. It fueled my conviction.

My brain injury made me focus on why I was in Japan — the job I had come there to do.

And I won. I had never skied that course before. But that day, I took home the gold medal.

I have had many accidents on the ski slopes from trying my hardest to do my best. I have suffered injuries in trying to be a winner. I cringe thinking about the brain injury or the time I broke my femur and when I tore my knee apart. I don't like to think about those times, but they are part of my journey.

Simon Bruty/Allsport

Portrait photo, page 5, Mike Powell/Allsport

Those memories are part of my "backpack of experience." And I pull from that backpack when I need protection, strength. When I need to trust in what I know because of what I have been through.

The young people in this book have shared their tremendous stories of strength and fortitude. In my opinion, they are all heroes — heroes born from adversity. Heroes who have struggled in ways many of us have never imagined. The insights I gained from their stories will go into my personal backpack.

You never know what experiences are going to prove to be the most powerful. It is my hope that these stories become part of the experiences that shape your life.

— *Picabo Street*

CLIMBING TO FREEDOM

*A climb to freedom doesn't have to be as high as a mountain. It can be
the height of a ladder firmly resting against an unwavering tree.
For Yvette S., grasping each rung of that ladder was a step toward freedom
from the damaging memories of sexual abuse. Standing at the top, she let
the sounds of rushing waters wash away the pain. On that ladder, she found
the strength to trust for the first time since the age of four.*

I was sexually abused by my grandfather on my stepdad's side.
It started when I was four years old and lasted until I was ten. I had to go
to his house after school every day because both of my parents worked
and they didn't want me coming home and staying by myself. When I
was really young, he would bribe me with candy. As I got older, he would
scare me with threats. I really understood at age eleven what he had done
to me, but I didn't tell anyone because I was afraid of him. That's when I
started getting into fights at school. I purposely wanted to get kicked out
of school so I would have to stop going to my grandfather's house.

Eventually, I did get expelled for fighting. Since I was getting old
enough to stay home alone, I started going to the school by my house.
This change put an end to the sexual abuse, but I was still angry — so I
kept fighting. Just a couple of months after attending my new school,
I was told to leave. So my parents put me in a Catholic school. My grandfather would drive by and watch me when I was outside at lunchtime.

Around that time I met a guy my age who lived right across the street
from the school. His family was part of a gang from California. I liked the
fact that he was in a gang. There were always kids at his house after school,
hanging around, smoking pot in his basement. So I started smoking pot.

Smoking pot helped me take away a little bit of the pain I held inside me. I was filled with hate and anger and I was sad every single day. My whole life felt so hopeless. I dealt with my fear and pain by constantly fighting with my family. On the outside, I blamed those fights on my family or my friends. On the inside, though, I blamed it on myself.

I went through a lot of friends during those years, almost like candy. I would try to trust them. But then they would do something that would stab me in the back. All my life, people used me. I wanted to trust people so badly. I would give my all to them — and it seemed I always got hurt in return. I didn't feel like there was anybody I could tell what I had been through.

I felt tough hanging out with gang members. And that felt good. I thought I could handle anything. When I was thirteen, I pulled a knife on a girl in the parking lot of another school. She was slamming my friend's gang and I heard about it, so I went to her school and put a knife up to her throat. I don't even know why I did it. I was just so angry with everybody. I was charged with assault for that incident and put on probation.

That night, I got into a huge fight with my parents. My mom yelled at me and asked me why I was acting so mean. That's when I let it all out. I just exploded. I told her how Grandpa had touched me. I told them how he would bribe me with candy. I told them the stuff he would say to me. I told them everything, even that I was doing drugs. It was such a painful day — for me, and for my parents.

My stepdad told me I was making up excuses to get myself out of trouble. It made me sad that he didn't believe me, but what was worse is that both my parents soon acted like I never said it, like it never happened — just swept it all under the rug. They knew what had happened, and they weren't doing anything to help me. So I still felt so alone.

As I moved up into high school, I kept on causing problems. I came to school intoxicated. I had started drinking a lot and smoking weed and that showed up in the urinalysis. Because of that, I was sent to Daybreak, a residential treatment facility.

I lived at Daybreak and went to school there. Being at Daybreak meant starting family therapy. During the sessions I felt like my family and I were putting up a front for the therapist. We acted like we were getting along as a family, but we weren't really talking to each other. It felt like no one was really addressing the issues that we knew were just beneath the surface.

While I was at Daybreak, they asked if I wanted to go on a weekend with Outward Bound in the mountains. It was going to be a group of eight girls who all had past experiences with family violence and sexual abuse. I didn't want to go at first, but something inside made me say yes, I would go. And I'm so glad I did.

At camp we did this activity where you have a partner and you fall backward toward that person, trusting that the person will catch you. It was so hard for me to hear someone say, "Come on, Yvette, you can trust me." People have said that to me in the past. But then they would end up stabbing me in the back. But somehow, that wasn't how it was at camp with my partner Michelle. I closed my eyes and thought, "Oh, my gosh," and I fell back. Before that exercise, I felt there was no one in the world I could trust like that. But Michelle was really there to catch me! It was an amazingly great feeling to be able to actually trust someone. It raised my spirits. It made me feel so happy.

Another exercise we did was called "Willow in the Wind." That's where you stand alone in the middle of a circle of people and you allow yourself to fall back into their hands. They catch you and push you up, and then you let yourself fall back again. I was really afraid of this exercise because it was scary not knowing where people were going to be touching me, or which way they were going to push me. But then I started thinking that if I could get myself to do it, it would be a big accomplishment. Once I started thinking about it positively, it felt okay for me to try it. I even started laughing when I was in the middle of the circle. It was so incredibly freeing to let other people catch me and push me to another set of hands that would also catch me.

No one dropped me. And no one scared me. And I was so happy I had given it a try.

Next, the leaders placed a wooden ladder against a tree. Once you climbed to the top of the ladder, you were supposed to let yourself fall back. Two lines of people at the bottom had their hands clasped together to catch you. I knew the ladder wasn't really that high, but it felt high as I was climbing. I had flashbacks in my head about not being able to trust anyone. When I finally stood at the top of that ladder, I blanked everything out of my head except for the sound of the river. At that moment I felt like I had no problems. I listened to the sound of the water rushing by. Flashbacks of sad times came into my head, but I let them get washed away by the sound of the water.

Then I closed my eyes and fell backward. When the people caught me, I was happier than I had ever been. I started to cry. It felt so good to give people a chance. It was shocking to me that they caught me. When I talk about it now, eight months later, I still want to cry about it.

The next day, we were supposed to do rock climbing. We had symbols painted on our faces before we started climbing to help give us strength. I had a horse painted on my face because it's such a beautiful, strong animal. We also carried pouches that had things that would help give us strength when we climbed. I had a bracelet my Grandma gave me with the Ten Commandments on it. I also had some colorful leaves.

With all these symbols, I carried a lot of strength with me as I was going to the top, even though one of my shoes almost fell off. When I made it to the top, I was filled with the beauty of that place. And as I looked around, I quietly decided I was going to leave the bad feelings that I didn't want inside of me any more right there. And I did — I left all the sexual abuse right there on top of that rock.

While I was at camp, I thought about a lot of people I had once thought were my friends. I realized those people never really were my friends — it was all about getting drugs and using one another. So when I came home, I let them go. I didn't tell them outright, or say anything hurtful to them. I just sort of stopped talking to them, and they stopped calling me.

I realized, too, that my parents had always cared for me. And I told them I was sorry for some of the things I had said and done to them. I can talk to my mom now, and we have a much better relationship. In a way, I'd say my mom and I are like best friends now. We make a real effort to talk more than argue about things. I also understand why my stepdad didn't believe me when I first told him about the sexual abuse. I knew it had to be hard for him to hear that his father would do something like that. He may not have believed me at first. But as time went on, he knew I was telling the truth — and he hurt like I did.

Now, I have true friends. The difference is that my friends now have respect for me. We hang around a lot, but it's not drugs or alcohol that is keeping us friends. We're open with each other. There are no secrets. Before Outward Bound, my ideas of friendship were more about just needing to have people around me, or thinking I needed to do drugs. We were just all using each other for our own reasons. But that's not how it is with me today. Today it's just about friendship.

Not too long ago, I didn't have much motivation or any real sense of my future. But now I know I can do things. I just put my mind to it —

and I know I can do it. I want to work with animals, so I am saving money to go to college. I was never like that before. Before, I just always dreamed about doing certain things, but I wasn't confident enough to do anything about making those dreams come true. Now I am actually making good things happen.

If I could climb that ladder and I could climb that rock — if I could let go of some of those feelings that were holding me back — I know I can do anything.

— Yvette S.

Survivors of Violence Recovery is a program designed to offer challenging group experiences that enhance cooperation and trust. The program's mission is to develop individual character, promote self-discovery and challenge students to cultivate self-reliance, leadership, fitness, compassion and service through exceptional wilderness education, among a safe and similar peer group. For more information, call Sian Hauver at 303-831-6974; write to Colorado Outward Bound School, 945 Pennsylvania Street, Denver, Colorado 80203; or visit www.cobs.org.

Daybreak-Princeton Girls Home is a long-term residential treatment center for adolescent girls that provides therapeutic services for children and their families from six months to one year. For more information, write 4121 S. Julian Way, Denver, Colorado 80236, or call 303-761-6773.

LEAVING THE GANG BEHIND

*Gang membership means instant brothers and immediate enemies.
It creates a sense of protection and a sense of security — but it's a false sense.
In reality, you're always looking over your shoulder. Although gang
membership doesn't have to be a life sentence, it takes tremendous courage
for a young man or woman to leave a gang to define his or her individual
identity. Seyha Leang found that courage during a thought-provoking
experience in the quiet of the wilderness. That's when he made the
decision to recapture his right to be his own man.*

Santa Anna, California, is a city of less than one million people and home to more than 120 gangs. Santa Anna has the highest number of gang-related homicides in the U.S. Most of the Asian kids my age in my neighborhood were in a gang, and there was a lot of peer pressure to join. I jumped into a gang when I was twelve years old.

That very same year, I was arrested on July 4 for possessing a pipe bomb. I was put on probation for six months. But at age twelve, I didn't really understand fully what that meant. So I started skipping curfew and hanging out with gang members, even though my probation restricted me from doing that. Since I violated probation, they put me in jail for one week. I didn't like jail — but as soon as I got out, I went back to messing with my homeboys and smoking pot.

When I was thirteen, I got into a fight and was kicked out of school. I wasn't even in the seventh grade — and here I was kicked out of school. It was a shock because I had never been punished like that at school. I was allowed to go back to school, but I didn't stop fighting. I really thought I needed to fight to prove myself and to solve my problems.

By the time I was fifteen, I was taking speed every day. If I didn't have money to buy it, I would steal a car stereo and sell that to get the money. One time, I was driving a stolen car with my friend, and the cops saw us pull out of a parking lot. I didn't want the cops to catch us, so we hit the gas and took off. We jumped out of the car while it was still moving and it hit another car. I saw the police catch my friend and I watched them beat him. It looked bad. I managed to hide for two hours behind a door in a garage while the police were looking for me. They came so close, but didn't find me there. Then I went to another homeboy's house. But when he took me back to my house, the police were waiting there. That time, I was locked up for six months.

During those six months, they tried sending me to a disciplinary camp. But I just couldn't stay out of trouble. Since I couldn't follow the camp rules — no fighting, no talking back — I was sent back down to juvenile detention. That was bad because I was put in a small cell. At camp, at least there were people I could talk to. At the juvenile hall, I was alone in my cell.

The counselors interviewed me and asked me why they should give me another chance and allow me to come back to camp. I said the words I knew they wanted to hear, so I felt like I talked them into letting me go back to camp.

When I first got back to the camp, I was doing well. But then I started acting up. Like a little kid. I would have outbursts and violent tantrums. I wanted to do the right things, but inside I was a time bomb, I just went off at anything or anyone that crossed me. So again, I was sent back to juvenile hall. Finally, after six months of going back and forth, my time was up, and I got to go home. I told myself I would never go back to camp or juvenile hall.

But in one week out, I was worse than ever.

By that time, I was starting to leave the neighborhood with my homeboys, and we were getting into fights at parties. It was hard on me because I was fifteen — the youngest hanging with the group — and I would get beat up bad. There would be shootings, too. I would come home bloody and bruised, and my mom would cry. But I never thought at all about her feelings. I would just yell at her because I thought she was giving me some kind of lecture.

I also started jacking cars to get stuff to sell so I could buy drugs, compact discs, and expensive clothes. And my older homeboys introduced me to guns.

The first time I held a gun, I was so happy. I felt powerful. I felt that gun earned me instant respect and put a fear out there for my enemies.

Before I was sixteen, I was doing crack cocaine. I did it a lot. I'd never sleep. I was always looking for it. Because of that addiction, I even began stealing from my mom. Even while I was doing it, I couldn't believe I would steal from my own mom. But I did.

One night, I was at a party with my homeboys, and we were planning on shooting a rival gang member. We were smoking weed and talking about the shooting. My homeboy who was leaving the party asked me for the gun, and I gave it to him. The guy ended up getting caught in a traffic violation, and the police found the gun. The cops found out it was mine. They came to the party and arrested me.

My probation officer was right there at the station when we got there. He was so mad. He even brought up charges from the past that he was holding because he hoped I was changing for the better. He said he wanted the judge to send me to Youth Authority (YA), which is a hardcore prison for teenagers.

The judge gave me one year, with an option for nine months if I was good. They didn't send me to YA, but they did send me to another camp. The first night I was there, I got into a fight, and they put me in confinement. I didn't like that at all. So I started acting right.

For a while, I was doing so well that they gave me furloughs — time off to visit my mom and my family. But when I got home, I would go right over to my homeboy's house and start smoking weed and looking for trouble. Then, when I got back to the camp, I would be drug tested — and I would be in trouble. Because of that, I was cuffed and sent back down to juvenile hall.

After I served my sentence, my probation officer enrolled me in Summit School, which is a correction and education facility for students on formal probation. He put me there because of the school's reputation for positively changing the hardest core students.

After I was there a little while, the school principal, Mr. Anderson, asked me if I wanted to be a part of a television show about teens and violence called "Teenfiles: Teens on Violence." The show picked eight youth, five boys and three girls, from different states, who all had a history of violence. I said yes.

Mr. Anderson and I flew from California to Colorado to meet the rest of the group. At first, I was nervous to leave my neighborhood. I had never been out of the city before. We were going to be part of a wilderness program called Educo that helps youth find inner strength by dealing with challenges that exist in the wilderness.

Once we landed in Colorado, we drove a few hours from the airport to the mountains. I had never been in the woods. The other camps I was in were part of the city. When we got to camp, I was just amazed at how pretty everything was. The mountains were amazing. The woods were great. They smelled so good. The air was fresh.

But most of all, it was really peaceful. You never had to look behind your back to see what was coming up on you. You could just walk anywhere.

There were these streams, and they were so cold that they made me feel numb. But I went in them anyway. It was a totally different kind of numb than what I felt when I was on drugs. I thought it was funny how cold that water was. I had never felt that cold in my life — but I felt really alive, too.

We did this Native American ritual of going under the water four times and, on the fourth time, picking up a rock from the bottom as a reminder of the fire inside us. I still have that rock. I keep it to remind me of that moment when I felt so clean and alive.

I felt like violence wasn't necessary in that environment. I didn't have to watch my back or worry that someone would shoot me for being Asian or being in the wrong neighborhood.

In nature there are a lot of different noises, and I could hear the birds. I saw deer tracks. And the stars at night were incredible. I had never seen stars like that before. At night, when it was quiet, and I was looking at the stars outside, or from inside my sleeping bag, I could think. In some ways, it was like I was really thinking clearly for the first time. Just letting myself think.

In jail or juvenile you need to pay attention to what's going on all the time. You can't just let your mind wander and think. You need to watch yourself. But at this camp, I started thinking about how I really could be doing better with my life. I knew I could be doing better stuff than gang banging.

That was the first time I ever thought like that.

All that thinking brought me to some changes in my life. When I came home, I started kicking it with my friends who weren't in gangs. These were the guys who didn't have enemies or belong to gangs. I already knew these guys pretty well, but hadn't spent much time with them because I was so involved with the gang. It was hard to change friends because it changed everything — the girls I went out with, the places I would go, the things I would do for fun.

We'd go to the movies together or walk on the beach. Some of the guys would walk with their girlfriends. It was a cool time. I felt comfortable. I wasn't worried about getting busted for anything because I wasn't

doing anything wrong. I still have to worry about rivals who don't know I have changed, but I don't really go to the places where they are so I don't really worry about it too much.

When my homeboys wanted me to come back to the gang, I told them I may be missing out by not being with them, but I knew there were better things for me. If I hung with them, there was a chance of getting hurt or getting in trouble again. And I knew I didn't want that. They respect me, so they left me alone. I still see them in the neighborhood and we talk, but I don't kick it with them anymore.

I will finish high school this year. I want to go to college. My probation officer is shocked at the changes I've made. This is the longest I have been out of trouble ever — and I want to keep it that way.

I am going to try to be a counselor for Educo in the summer.

I loved the wilderness, the mountains, all that stuff. The wilderness changed me. I don't have an ugly heart anymore.

— *Seyha Leang*

Educo School of Colorado conducts wilderness-based programs that foster wisdom, leadership, compassion, and a sense of purpose in individuals around the world. Participants leave the program with heightened self-esteem, new skills, and an awareness of the significant role they play in the future of the world.

For more information, contact David Miller, executive director, 800-332-7340; write to Educo, 406 North College Avenue, Fort Collins, Colorado 80524; or visit www.educointernational.org.

PUSHING SICKNESS ASIDE

*For twelve-year-old Nathan Brainard, a routine check-up at the
doctor's office evolved into an overnight stay and an introduction to his
hospital home for the next two years. Over many long, quiet days, propped up
by pillows in his hospital bed, he would stare out the window, longing to be
a normal teenager. But twice a year, Nathan's days sped by — filled with
swimming, rock climbing, hiking, laughing. On those days, he became
a boy with more energy and hope than he had thought possible.*

I was diagnosed with leukemia on Good Friday. It was a half-day of
school, and I went to the doctor's office for a check-up. By that evening,
I was staying in the hospital.

I originally went to the doctor's that day because of something one
of my teachers had said. I was wild when I was in sixth grade, and one
day when I was being really disruptive, the teacher decided to call my
mom. During the call, the teacher made a comment that I looked green.
None of us knew what in the world she was talking about. No one in my
family thought I looked green. But my mom decided I should go to the
doctor anyway.

The doctor examined me and said everything looked fine and I was
free to go.

As soon as he said that, I was up, out of that room, and down the
hallway. But as my mom started to leave, the doctor said maybe we
should do one more test. I came all the way back, and they did a finger
prick. The nurse blotted it on a slide and said it didn't look right, so we
tried it again. And she said it still didn't look right. The doctor said he
wanted us to go down to the hospital. At that point, I still wasn't thinking anything was wrong. I thought they had somehow just messed up on
the blood test.

From the doctor's office, we went downtown to the hospital — to the oncology/hematology department. That was the first time I had ever been in there. Little did I know I would be spending quite a bit of time there. That day, they drew some more blood, and we had to wait for a long time. Then the doctor and two nurses came out to talk to my mom and me. All of a sudden, my mom just started crying, and I was freaked out. She called my dad, hysterical, and told him to get down to the hospital. I was completely clueless, my mom was freaking out, my dad couldn't figure out what was going on, and the doctor and nurses started leading me upstairs. They were throwing words like "cancer" and "leukemia" around, but I was in sixth grade. Those words didn't mean anything to me. Later that night, I started to realize I was sick. I didn't know what I was sick with, but I knew it was serious and that I shouldn't plan on going home any time soon. I was so confused that I didn't really know what to feel.

From that point on, I never went back to sixth grade. For the rest of the school year and the whole summer, I was in the hospital. Three days after the diagnosis, I found out I had chicken pox for the second time. I had to be put in an isolation room. I had never been to a hospital before, and that isolation room was really bad for a first impression. It made me think that was how it was going to be all the time — a little room all by myself. And the few people who could visit had to be in full scrubs and facemasks because of the chicken pox. It got so boring, I would hold my breath until I got the buzzer to go off on the breath monitor — just to get someone to come talk to me. But after a week or two, I was getting over the chicken pox and was taken out of the isolation room and moved to the fourth floor. This is where my new home would be and where they started the real heavy chemotherapy.

The chemotherapy had some terrible side effects. Physically, I became so weak from both the medication and the disease that I couldn't even roll over. I would have pillows propping me up sideways so I could sleep.

One day, about ten months later, two nurses asked if I wanted to go to camp. I was bald. I was tiny — my weight had gone from 120 pounds to 95 pounds — and I felt real sick. But as soon as they mentioned it, I knew I wanted to go. When my parents said I could, we went ahead and made plans. I was really excited to be doing something that sounded so normal — and so exciting.

But while all of us kids who were waiting to go to camp crowded the hospital hallway, waiting for the bus that would take us to camp, I started to get scared. It was a combination of being that far from home and the hospital, being away from my parents, and then lots of little things — a fear of trying new things, of being around new people. The anxiety really hit me. But my parents said that if anything happened, they would be there in a few hours.

That helped, so I got on the bus.

On the bus ride, I was very quiet. I sat in the corner in the front and didn't say anything. It was a long bus ride. Once we got into Breckenridge, we started heading up a long, steep dirt road. Then all of a sudden out of the trees comes a large log cabin. It was three stories high, with large windows, and a huge wood deck that went around most of it. We pulled up right in front of it and our counselor said, "Here we are." I was really excited — until I noticed he was pointing at a little and very old cabin sitting across the lake.

We had arrived at camp at lunch time. It was the first time I got a taste of how they do lunch at camp. They threw jumbo jars of peanut butter and jelly on the table, and huge loaves of bread and told us to have at it. It might not sound like much, but that was really fun after eating hospital food. They definitely made sure you didn't go hungry. PB&J's were way better than hospital food.

Camp was fun because you got to hang out with kids who were not just kind of like you, but with those who were exactly like you. And you got to do it outside a hospital setting.

Very, very few kids actually got sick at camp to a point where they had to leave early. I remember there were times, in the hospital, I was so sick and sore I could barely move.

But for the five years I've gone to camp, I couldn't wait to get up and get going. I was so excited. I would get out of bed early in the morning with my stuff packed and ready to go. It was like you were so sick, but you looked forward to doing something so much that your sickness didn't matter.

There was this pond in the middle of the camp where we would go swimming. Even in the summer the water was frigid cold, but we didn't care. We would dive in. We would have so much fun. We would throw the counselors, or anyone who got close enough, into the water. One night at each session of camp, we would have in-depth conversations about our illnesses and what happened. But other than that, we very seldom talked about being sick. When we were at camp, we didn't feel sick — so our illness was the last thing we wanted to talk about.

While I was in the hospital, I questioned if I could ever do anything again. When you're sitting in bed, you don't know if you are ever going to be able to play again, let alone when. The last thing you'd ever think you'd be doing is scaling a rock wall or swimming in a mountain lake. But when I was at camp, it seemed like I could do anything.

When I got home, I would be so sore that I usually needed a day or two just to recover. But I didn't care. I couldn't wait to go the next time.

While I was in the hospital I spent a lot of time by myself. I had a lot of time to think about my disease. I became quiet and reserved, definitely not the same boy who was disrupting class in the sixth grade. Before camp, I was only concerned with myself. I never realized there were other kids going through the same thing I was.

For the next two and a half years, I was in and out of — but mostly in — the hospital. I went to camp a total of five times, two times a year during those years. Each trip I became more vocal on the bus trip. Toward the end they just about couldn't shut me up. I would chit-chat all the time.

Six years ago, at age fifteen, I was considered officially cured of leukemia. I don't have cancer and I don't go to camp any more, but I still enjoy going back to that area. Only now, I teach other people what I learned there. The first time I ever rock climbed was at camp — on a real rock climbing wall just outside of Breckenridge. It was kind of scary because you were on your little fingertips and toes and you were way up there, but it's a short easy pitch.

This past summer, I took four or five trips out there to teach other people how to rock climb. I got my parents to rock climb. I took my four cousins and several friends. And my aunt and uncle made me promise I would take them rock climbing next summer. I take everyone to the exact spot I learned to climb. And now I am passing it on to others. That is kind of cool.

— *Nathan Brainard*

The Children's Hospital of Denver offers a winter and summer Wilderness Adventure for teenagers age 12 to 18 who have had treatment for cancer. Oncology nurses join the staff of the Breckenridge Outdoor Education Center to provide a four- to five-day wilderness experience with a variety of outdoor activities.

For more information, call the oncology department, 303-861-6740, and ask for the nurse who organizes the teen wilderness program; or visit www.tchden.org.

Photograph © John Fielder 2001

A LIFE-CHANGING
PERFORMANCE

At seventeen, Matt Thompson was overflowing with confidence. He was on his own path, heading toward a career in acting. Then came the car accident that literally threw him off course. Losing control of his car on a patch of ice, Matt was thrown forty yards from his vehicle — almost half the length of a football field. When he awoke from a coma, he found he had to relearn the very basics of life — how to walk, how to feed himself, how to speak. He spent several weeks teaching himself to tie his own shoes again. His passion for acting dimmed. But as Matt later discovered, through the safe environment of a camp for the brain injured, his desire to act had not been extinguished.

At sixteen, I could have been called an overachiever. I won awards for my acting performances. I walked away with honors at forensic meets. I was becoming a strong singer. I was set with the idea that I would to go to Northwestern University as soon as I graduated from high school, because it has a great theater program. I was carefree and happy about everything. None of the world's problems mattered to me. I was in acting, choir, getting good grades, and I had great friends.

But that changed in an incident that I will never be able to remember.

I lived in a small town in eastern Colorado. One night, four days after my seventeenth birthday, I took a road trip with my friend Regan to a bigger town an hour away from my home. We were venturing out to get some film developed at a one-hour place and to just kick around for a bit. On our way home, without warning, the weather turned bad. We were driving through an ice storm that came up out of nowhere.

I have no memory of what happened to us on the way home, but the police report says I hit a patch of ice, slid to the right, tried to correct it, hit another patch of ice, and lost control of the car. The vehicle rolled over twice. Because I wasn't wearing a seat belt, I was launched through the driver's side window. My head hit the pavement forty yards from the car.

Regan was bruised, but she wasn't badly hurt. She ran to the road and waved down help. Regan tells me I was having convulsions while waiting for the ambulance. She was really scared.

When we got to the hospital, they said they weren't really equipped to handle severe trauma injuries. They wanted to send me to Denver on a helicopter, but the weather made it too dangerous to fly. They raced me to Denver via ambulance. The drive took three hours.

The doctors told my parents that with the way my head hit the ground, my brain rebounded against my skull. Through CAT scans and MRI they found three separate half-inch tears in my brain.

I was in a coma for two weeks.

I really don't really remember waking up. I slept a lot. Some days I slept as much as twenty-two hours. When staff members came in my room, they would say my name several times to help me remember who I was.

I wasn't ready to start relearning how to live for a couple of months. I had to start from the beginning. Every day, for most of the day, I was in physical, occupational, and speech therapy.

At first, I was in a wheelchair. My muscles didn't know how to walk. I had double vision. I would forget what I had eaten for breakfast five minutes after I finished it. I didn't even have a clue that I had just eaten. I was thinking, "How can I focus on getting better, when I can't even remember what day it is two minutes after they tell me?"

I became withdrawn — just balled up in silence. I wasn't deliberately trying to hide my feelings, but I wasn't up to expressing what I felt. My brain was too busy with trying to heal.

After many months of intensive therapy and tutoring, I was walking and talking, so I returned to school for my senior year. It was really hard. My memory was bad, so I was struggling in the classroom like I never had before. Some of my friends acted weird around me.

For a long time people didn't know how to treat me. They thought I was breakable. That made me mad. I thought, "You know what, I am not breakable. I am still a person and you should just deal with it." People could be demeaning. They would treat me as if I was "the little injured child." I wanted to scream at them, "Yes, I have changed, but I am still me."

Then I learned from one of my therapists about the Brain Injury Association's camp. She said I would be in the wilderness and expected to do the same things that people without brain injuries would do, but that I would be with a bunch of people who had brain injuries. It wouldn't be competitive and they would make sure I was safe, but it would challenge me physically. In fact, the camp staff told me they wanted me

to be a counselor since my injury was less severe than others who would be at camp. That sounded cool, so I decided to go.

My parents drove me to camp on a Saturday. They tried to hide their feelings, but I knew they were nervous about leaving me at this camp. And I tried to hide the fact that I was nervous, too. I didn't know what to expect. But as soon as I got there, I felt good.

I grew up in the plains of Colorado, not the mountains, so to be in the mountains was absolutely beautiful. The scenery was spectacular. It was fulfilling to me. From the very start, it just felt right.

I had never been around other people with brain injuries. I didn't have a roommate while I was in the hospital, and my therapies were always individual. So I didn't have much experience with other people who had brain injuries. For the first time, I was talking with other people who were struggling with the same things I was struggling with. When I met people who had to overcome larger hurdles than the ones I faced, it made me feel so grateful for what I had and how far I had come. At camp, they called the counselors "buddies." I was eighteen and I was a buddy to someone who was thirty-four. But with traumatic brain injury, a person really isn't their physical age anymore, so helping someone who was older wasn't really a big deal. It just felt great to help someone else and forget about my own problems for a while.

One evening after dinner, there was a group of us hanging out in the kitchen. I started singing quietly to myself. The person next to me started quietly singing along with me. That sort of energized me. So I started singing louder. Pretty soon a bunch of us were singing "Jeremiah was a Bullfrog." It was so much fun and made me feel amazing inside. I surprised myself.

That moment in that kitchen — with so many people singing and feeling happy — was a breakthrough for me. For the first time in a long, long time, I saw potential for my life.

On the second-to-last day of camp, we were asked to do a skit. The staff handed us some common camp stuff, like oars and flashlights, and told us those were our props.

As soon as I grabbed that oar, my body recalled the feelings I had had about acting, before the accident. I was energized at the thought of performing. It hit me that I hadn't done this in so long. And through it all, I knew I was safe in that camp environment because no one was judging me. It didn't matter to them whether our skit was good, or if I was good. It was just about getting up in front of the group and doing it. And since they weren't judging me, I thought I shouldn't judge myself, either. So I didn't judge myself, and felt good about myself again.

Once I started the skit, I got totally into it. My passion for acting — that desire that had burned inside me so strongly before the accident — was once again in full force. At that moment, I realized that I had pushed acting out of my life for far too long. I felt that familiar craving for approval from an audience. I did a big cheesy bow at the end of our skit. I drank in the applause. I loved every minute of it.

And now, I'm back on track. Yes, my plans have changed a bit because I need to adapt to my situation. But I am once again committed to acting. And I'm once again committed to going to college. Instead of going to Northwestern, I will be going to the University of Northern Colorado in Greeley because it has great resources for disabled students. And I accept the fact that in some areas I need some help. My reading has been slowed, so books and lectures on tape really help me learn. When I use them, I can take notes at my own pace. The school has a great tutoring program. And I've learned that I can ask for help when I need it. I'm okay with that now.

My experiences from the wreck have changed me in so many ways, but I want to be treated like nothing had ever happened. Each day I like to live my life in a way that helps people understand how they can truly help someone who is disabled — how to help them take on challenges with dignity.

Before the accident I used to think I could do anything as far as theater and acting were concerned. But now I think, "You know what, I am not limited by anything." I feel like I have been through a lot in my life and I could do anything if I set my mind to it.

My brain is still working on repairing itself. So what if I don't have dreams when I sleep? When I'm awake, I daydream about being on stage.

I see it in my mind. I know I can make it happen.

—Matt Thompson

The Brain Injury Association of Colorado works with camp facilities in the state to provide outdoor adventure challenge experiences for adults with brain injuries. In 2000, that partnership included Easter Seals, which provides all staff for activities ranging from traditional camp fires to adaptive golf, and the Breckenridge Outdoor Education Center. BIAC provides financial assistance for camp to its members through a grant from the Horowich Foundation. BIAC also recruits volunteers, including nurses, to assist campers with BOEC activities, such as rock climbing and rafting.

For further information about the BIAC Outdoor Adventure Challenge Program, call BIAC, 800-955-2443 or 303-355-9969; write to BIAC, 4200 West Conejos, Suite 524, Denver, Colorado 80204; or visit www.biacolorado.org, www.boec.org, or www.eastersealsco.org.

CHAOS TO SERENITY

Sandy Rivera grew up in a household characterized by chaos. While other children might run to the front door to greet their father upon his return home from a day of hard work, Sandy and her siblings would retreat and hide. After her older brother and sister, as teenagers, each made the move to leave home, Sandy felt alone in the battleground of her home. Eventually she left all that was frenetic, yet familiar, in California, to finish high school in the mountains of Colorado. There she connected with the spirit of her great-grandmother and found the courage to define a life without violence.

My father was a heavy drinker and very abusive to my mother, my brother, my older sister, and me. There was a lot of hitting, yelling, and violence in my home. He would hit my mom. My brother and sister and I would try to stop him. But then he would turn to hitting us. He would scream mean, nasty stuff at us.

Although we are one family there was a great division between my older sister, older brother, and me and my three younger sisters. I am five years older than the oldest of my three younger sisters. He was a different man with the younger set. He was kind to them.

My dad had this old Toyota truck and we knew when he turned the corner if he stepped on the gas too much, he was drunk. When my brother and sister were still at home and we heard that truck squeal, we would automatically run to our bedrooms and pretend we were asleep. We didn't care that we were missing dinner. We just didn't want to see him.

My older sister ran away when she was sixteen. A year later my brother left when he was fifteen. I felt really alone.

After my brother left I never wanted to be home. My mom would argue with me because I would come home late, but I never wanted to come home at all because of my dad.

At that time I was part of a group called I Have a Dream Foundation, which helps kids succeed in school. This kind group wanted to help me and I just pushed them aside because I had an attitude. One day, when I was fifteen years old, I was talking, with attitude, to the program coordinator. I think she could see my pain, even though I was acting tough, and out of nowhere, she started to cry while she was talking to me. It took me by total surprise. It was the first time I ever felt someone really wanted to go out of her way to help me.

She helped me transfer to another middle school so I could have a fresh start. I wanted to do things right this time since I saw she cared about me. I tried to be really good, and I was good through middle school. I really tried to do well. But as soon as I hit high school my bad attitude was back.

In high school I was doing drugs and dragging friends of mine into doing drugs with me. By this time, I was feeling so much rage and hate toward my father and everyone else. On the surface though, I tried to act like everything was "peachy" and I was happy doing drugs, and that I could handle it all, acting like nothing hurt me. But inside I was negative. The rage was building inside of me.

One day, the program coordinator caught up to me and said she wanted to talk to me about making another change in my life. She told me about Eagle Rock.

Escape for me came when I found out about Eagle Rock School in Estes Park, in the Rocky Mountains of Colorado. Eagle Rock is a unique school, taking in kids from all over. It's for young people who are not experiencing success in their current school setting. I interviewed and was accepted to start school in Colorado in the fall.

I fell in love with Eagle Rock — the mountains, the fresh air, the fresh start.

Each new class of students leaves the main school area to camp in the wilderness for 23 days. I was calm about the whole idea and thought, "I can hang for 23 days without toilet paper. I can hang with no showering." And then they started making us chop up wood and teaching about what stuff to put in our backpacks. Then came the day I threw on this 80-pound pack and started walking with the group. I was scared.

I have never been out in the woods that long. I had never been camping, only to shooting ranges in the mountains. Here I was going to be camping in a little tiny tent.

Sometimes it was hard and I would want to quit, and when I felt like that I thought about my great-grandma. In my room at home, I have a picture of my mom's grandma. It's a black and white picture of just her face. Her hair is in braids. She's wearing a string of beads. She looks straight at you. I never met her. I just know her by that picture. For some reason during wilderness I felt connected to her. I would go off walking by myself and when the wind blew I could hear her beads.

I would cry because I believed she was there, taking care of me. I felt really loved. I felt like a whole person. I never felt like that before. When that wind blew and I heard the sounds of the beads, I dropped to my knees and I started praying to her to look after me and to protect me and to thank her for being there with me. And I closed my eyes. And I got this feeling. It was the first time I felt that feeling — not empty. Not ashamed any more. After that I started praying to her every day.

One time in the wilderness I fainted because I was dehydrated. The instructors put me in the tent. I could feel the wind blow the tent and in Spanish I heard, "Míja, levántate" which means "Get up, my child." I was looking around and thought, "Where did that come from?" I got up and started walking around and after that I didn't feel sick anymore. I knew in my heart that it was my great-grandma telling me in a loving way to get up. I felt so peaceful and calm inside — a new feeling after growing up in a house filled with chaos and ridicule.

After that I was on a roll in the wilderness. I laughed more. I smiled a lot. I was cooking for everybody. I realized my grandma was always with me in spirit. I felt incredible.

After the wilderness experience I discovered I am just Sandy Rivera, period. I am free to be whomever I want to be. One day I may choose to be the goofy Sandy and one day I may be the serious Sandy, but I always go back to the calm, mature Sandy. And I like that. People say I am mature for someone who's only seventeen.

Rivers have smooth stones, but they start out as sharp stones. To me, I was that pointy, jagged stone that no one would want to hold. But if you pick up a stone from the water, it is nice and smooth and you want to hold in your palm. That stone, though, had to go a long way with rolling and tumbling in the water to smooth out. And I think now that I have tumbled. I am that smooth stone. I am the smooth stone you want to hold in your hand.

I was a spiky stone from the experiences in my household. I believe the support I have at Eagle Rock is the water washing and smoothing me. The experience I had in the wilderness is the tumbling I needed to help make me smooth.

Eagle Rock didn't change me. They helped me, but it was me who figured it out. The opportunity out in the wilderness opened me up to make changes in my life. In my thoughts.

I feel clean inside now. I have accepted who my dad is and that we may never have a strong bond because he is not ready to change. I now know I will never be alone because I can close my eyes and remember the feeling of my great-grandmother's spirit within me, protecting me, talking to me peacefully. Helping me to feel peace.

— Sandy Rivera

Eagle Rock School is a year-round, tuition-free, ungraded residential high school providing personalized learning experiences to approximately a hundred high-school-aged students from diverse backgrounds. The students are characterized as those for whom success has been elusive. Each student operates from an individualized learning plan. Emphasis is given to learning to live and work and create a community environment.

For more information, write Eagle Rock School and Professional Development Center, 2750 Notaiah Road, P.O. Box 1770, Estes Park, Colorado 80517; call 970-586-0600 or 303-442-7655; or visit www.eaglerockschool.org.

RUNNING AROUND,
BREATHING DEEPLY

*At thirteen, Jennifer Hoag knew she was destined to die during
an asthma attack. She was absolutely sure her life would end one day while
she gasped and struggled for air, with no one around who would
know how to help her. That belief was challenged and ultimately
erased in one week in the Colorado wilderness.*

Not being able to breathe feels desperately confining. I've had lots of
asthma attacks in my life, and each one is as scary as the one before. I start
gasping for air, gulping for oxygen. My breaths become choppy, and I feel
like my lungs have stopped working. I grab for my medication. And after
one or two very long minutes, the medication starts helping. Finally, I can
take a deep breath. I'm exhausted by that point, but I can breathe.

I was diagnosed with asthma when I was five years old. From that
point on, until I was thirteen, my mom did everything necessary to take
care of my condition. She knew my medications, dosages, and schedule.
Every year when school started, she talked to the school nurse and to my
teachers about my needs. During those years, I was completely hands-off
about my disease and my medication. I was just there. Medicated.

Because I was so young when my mom started taking care of my
asthma needs, we fell into a routine — one that lasted seven years, until
I went to camp.

My mom tried to control my environment as much as possible to keep
me from having to suffer from an attack. I never went into our backyard
to look at the stars because the pollen count is higher at night, and pollen
can trigger an attack. I never stayed all night at a slumber party or spent

the night away from my mom. Each school year started with a note to my teachers from the doctor about what I could and couldn't do at recess.

My room at home was a spotless, clean bubble. My mattress and pillow were covered in plastic to keep them from getting dusty. The vent for the heater was wrapped in cheesecloth to screen out dust particles. All but a few of my stuffed animals were kept in another room because they would attract dust. I never left my dirty clothes in my room because they held the day's dust, pollen, and air pollution. The window was never opened.

When I was thirteen years old, our family doctor told my mom about the American Lung Association's Champ Camp, a camp for kids with asthma. My mother told me about it, and I immediately wanted to go. I knew there would be people there who would understand what it means to be an asthmatic. The doctors I worked with did a great job of talking about all the things happening in my lungs, but they couldn't feel the way I felt. At Champ Camp, though, I imagined talking to girls my age about asthma. People who would understand what I was feeling. People who would understand my restrictions, my fears.

I had really wanted to go to Champ Camp so badly, but nothing prepared me for what I saw when I arrived. It was like walking into another universe. To me, the whole camp was one big, frightening dust puddle.

I was shocked to see the cabin where I would be living. The mattresses weren't covered. The windows were open. I stood in the middle of the floor, feeling panicked about living under these conditions with all these other people for a whole week. Our counselors gave us each a T-shirt with a camp logo on it. We were told we would have to wear these shirts all week. I couldn't imagine how I was going to survive wearing a shirt the whole week that would be getting dirtier each day. I couldn't even imagine having dirty clothes in my room because they had the day's dirt on them.

As it turned out, that T-shirt was just the beginning of the changes I experienced that week. At home, my mom gave me my medication at specific times. But at camp, the counselors told me I would take my medication at meal times. That was shocking news because there was a three-hour time difference between when I usually would take my medicine and when we would be having breakfast at camp. I truly believed I was going to die from an attack during that gap of three hours. I just didn't think I could take my medicine any differently than the way my mom had me take it — and survive.

For the first four days, I cried every morning at breakfast. I was so sure I was going to have an attack that would kill me because of how different everything was.

On top of the fact that my medications were being given to me at different times than I was used to, I was forced to do more physical activity than I had ever done. I had always been afraid to run too much because I thought I wouldn't be able to breathe. At camp, they wanted us to learn what it was like to run — to run a mile!

On Wednesday of that week, the counselors told me I had to go on a hike with the group after lunch. I was dragging, and it was hard for me to keep up. I was tired and missing my mom. My counselor took hold of my hand to encourage me. But then it started to rain and we all crowded close together under a gazebo. I knew rain made the pollen come out, so I was sure I was going to have an asthma attack. I huddled close to the nurse and I started crying. When it stopped raining, the counselors had us run back to our cabins. By that time, I was terrified and sobbing hysterically. But since I had cried for most of camp, the counselors just consoled me like they always had. They were used to it. They had to do it every day.

When we got back to the cabin, it smelled so badly from all the wet clothes being dumped on the floor. I sat slumped on my bed and slowly changed into dry clothes. Instead of eating dinner in the mess hall with everyone, I ate with the doctors in the medical clinic and stayed there for a while that night. The medical staff reassured me that I was all right, but I figured with all the stuff that went down, this would be the day they would have to send me home in a pine box. I couldn't stop thinking about it. But nothing happened. Finally, I went back to my cabin and went to bed.

That night, the boys raided our cabin — so we chased them outside. After we came back in, I was sure that the dust all over my pajamas would give me an asthma attack. Frantically, I told my counselor I had to take a shower. But she wouldn't let me. She told me we only take showers after swimming and that I should just go to bed. I was terrified. I crawled into my sleeping bag thinking, "Oh my God. This is it. I am going to die."

Some time in the middle of that night, I woke up and thought about all that had happened that day.

It dawned on me that all the things that scared me about camp were really no big deal. For four days I had lived an opposite life from my life at home. I was roughing it. The camp was dirty, damp, dusty — and I was still breathing. There was no television or radio to hang out with. I was hiking and swimming. I was living in the wilderness, with other people. I was on a different schedule with my medications and I was doing fine.

I was still homesick, but I was living among the flowers and the trees and wasn't going to die at that moment from my asthma. I realized that I had two days left at camp, which still felt like an eternity being away from my mom, but I realized I was okay. For the first time, I thought that maybe I wasn't going to die at camp after all.

When I woke up the next morning, I felt different. It was a new feeling — a feeling of hope. I felt unburdened from worry. The counselors even commented on how I wasn't crying at breakfast. Instead of crying, I smiled. And I joined the other girls in doing practical jokes on the counselors. I even came up with a new prank myself, and they called me "Genius."

Before that time, I had just wanted to be by myself at camp. Or I wanted to hang with the doctors. When they wouldn't let me, I would just write and doodle. But on that Thursday, I came around and started goofing with the other girls. They were so nice to me. In fact, the girls in the cabin told me they were going to give me a surprise later that day. That night, they introduced me to a boy named Galen. He was my surprise — my date for the barn dance.

I wore one girl's denim mini-skirt and a different girl's denim jacket to the barn dance that night. I had never swapped clothes with anyone before. I used hairspray. I had never used hairspray before. And the girls helped me put on make-up. I had never done that before, either. I hadn't done any of those things because I had been so sure I would be allergic to those products and would get an asthma attack from them.

That night, we danced until we were sweaty. We ran up and down the dirt road outside. I had dust all over me. I was so distracted with the good time I was having, that I wasn't even worried. It was such a wonderful feeling. It was exciting to feel like I finally fit in — like I had arrived. I played hard and I slept well. It was the first night I didn't wake the doctor up to take my medication.

My mom says that when I came home from Champ Camp, I was a completely different person. She was surprised at my change in attitude. I explained I wasn't going to die if I didn't take a shower before bed or if I slept with the window open. I told her it felt really good sometimes to go out back before bed, to sit and look at the stars.

In the fall, I insisted on going outside at recess. And I decided to run track at school. Sometimes I would have to stop running because of my breathing, but I joined the team anyway. At first my mom was worried about my new attitude, but then she saw I was doing okay. We started to talk more instead of me just listening to her directions about asthma. I am really happy we made that change. Both my mom and I know she did what she had to in the beginning to keep me safe, but now we both know that I can live a normal life even with having asthma.

That week at camp was a turning point in my life. My deep fears led me to a complete emotional breakdown while I was there. I realized that even though I was one of the worst asthmatics at camp, I didn't have to see myself that way all the time. I really was just one of the girls.

Instead of living for my asthma, I realized I could live with my asthma. I could stop seeing myself as an asthmatic and see myself as Jennifer, a person with asthma.

To this day, I use the lessons I learned at camp to help me manage my disease, to give me courage to try new things, and to remind myself that just because something is done differently does not mean it's wrong.

— *Jennifer Hoag*

The American Lung Association's Champ Camp provides children with asthma with an opportunity to enjoy a week-long, traditional summer camp experience. Doctors, nurses, respiratory therapists, and counselors supervise campers twenty-four hours a day to ensure they have fun in a safe, learning environment. The primary goal of the camp is to provide children with tools for proper asthma management.

For more information, write the American Lung Association of Colorado, 1600 Race Street, Denver, Colorado 80206; call 303-388-4327 or 800-LUNG-USA (800-586-4872); or visit www.alacolo.org.

REMEMBERING MY FATHER

Chuck Taylor was a fifty-one-year-old father and husband.
He loved to race through loops on a roller coaster with his nine-year-old son,
John, at a local amusement park, or casually review papers at his office, while
John discussed computers with him. He was happy. He was healthy.
Everything was great. Until the night that Chuck's cry for help sliced the
silence of the early morning hours. Short of breath, gasping for air, he held his
chest. His wife tried CPR while their daughter called 911. But Chuck died less
than an hour later. Meanwhile, John slept through the chaos of sirens and
flashing lights, fire engines and an ambulance that lined his normally quiet
street. Each year since that night, John joins fifty-five other children in the
mountains for a weekend at camp — a weekend to hike, canoe, fish, and
remember in nature those they have lost.

My sister Carly woke me up at 6:30 that morning to tell me my dad was sick. I didn't really know what was going on until I went to the hospital. The hospital smelled stale. It was cold and very quiet. Then I saw my mom, and she was crying — crying hard. I knew things were bad. After I talked to her, she helped me go into a "quiet room" to kiss my dad and say good-bye. He was so still and so pale. It really scared me. But I don't think it really hit me that my dad was dead.

For a long time after that, I couldn't concentrate. Kids in the neighborhood tried to take my mind off of it. They would get me to come out and play street hockey. And I would try — but I couldn't even skate. My legs would just shake, and I couldn't even think straight.

Looking back on it now, I was kind of quiet that whole first year. I just didn't know what to say about missing my dad and how I was feeling inside. My mom made several attempts to try to get me to talk, but I kept it all inside. That's when a good friend told my mom about Camp Comfort. It sounded like a pretty good time with swimming and hiking. I knew I was going to be with other kids who had lost someone they loved, but it didn't sound like we would be crying all the time, so I said I would go.

My mom drove me to camp. My mom and I weren't talking much during the drive. I was thinking it would be good to get away from home for a little while.

Everyone who came to camp was asked to bring a picture or something that reminded them of the person they cared about who had died. When all the kids and counselors got together in the main building we sat down in a circle and shared about the picture we had brought. Some kids had stories to tell. Others just passed around a picture and didn't say much. When it came to my turn to talk, words and stories about my dad just spilled out. I talked about how he died. How he once was a body guard for television star Valerie Bertinelli. How he was once a security guard for the Los Angeles Dodgers. How we went hiking and camping in the mountains. I felt like I was showing off, but it felt so good to talk about my dad. I hadn't talked like that, or about him, in a long, long time. I guess I felt safe and I knew the other kids would understand. When we were done and we went to our cabins, we taped all the pictures up on the cabin walls and really decorated the place. I liked that.

That night, everybody at camp met at the campfire and we made up funny skits and had a talent show under the stars. It was a blast.

The first year I went to Camp Comfort, we planted a tree. It was just a little sapling of a tree, but we tied ribbons with the names and memories of someone we'd lost around its branches and trunk. That tree was wrapped up in ribbons! It was really colorful and cool to watch the ribbons waving in the wind. And it was really hard to feel alone when right in front of us was a little colorful tree with all those ribbons blowing. The next two summers I went to camp, I would go look at that tree to see how it was growing. The ribbon was faded, but I could still read my dad's name and the names on the other ribbons that were tied on by my friends. It made me really remember my dad.

Another year that I went to camp, we stood on this bridge that crosses a large river. The bridge was crowded with kids. Each of us was holding a fresh carnation. We wrote messages to the people we lost on leaves and rolled the leaves around the stems of the flowers. The group leader read us a poem and we all said, "we remember" at certain parts. Then, we had a moment of silence. After that, some kids said something out loud about the people they had lost, and some kids silently said a prayer, but everyone was thinking about the friend whom they had lost. Then, we

Photograph © John Fielder 2001

dropped our flowers from the bridge into the river. It was beautiful to see all the flowers floating; all the different colors.

I said a prayer for my dad on that bridge. I didn't feel like crying just then. But some kids were crying, and that was okay. It was cool because they knew they could cry and not be alone. With fifty other flowers floating right next to theirs, they weren't alone right then — and they knew they never would be.

There is always someone in the world feeling pain or sorrow, and we can all help each other through it. Our counselors helped the kids — and the kids helped other kids, too.

When my mom picked me up that first year, I couldn't stop talking about camp. I told her what we did, the new friends I made, and for the first time in a long time, I really talked about how I felt inside.

Each year at camp, I take some time to go to one particularly special place. It's a place where you can see everything at once: the open field, the forest, the river, and the valley. My dad loved the outdoors. It's awesome being someplace I know my dad would love. I always find some time to come to this spot to look around at everything. And when I do, I feel like my dad is with me at that place.

I plan to keep coming to camp for as long as I can because I have friends here that I see once a year. And when I can't come any longer because I am too old, I plan to come as a counselor because I know what it's like to lose someone you love. It hurts. But kids need to know they are never alone when it hurts.

I'll visit this special spot forever.

— John Taylor

Mount Evans Hospice and Home Health Care established Camp Comfort in 1995 to meet the needs of grieving children. Camp Comfort, a weekend bereavement camp for children grieving the death of a family member or friend, meets each year in the summer in the mountains of Colorado. More than fifty children and fifty volunteers gather to share memories and begin the journey of healing after a painful loss of someone they love.

The children participate in a mix of sharing and learning through workshops led by professional counselors. They also enjoy traditional camp activities, such as swimming, boating, and fishing. Each child is given valuable one-on-one time with an adult volunteer "buddy," who provides support and friendship throughout the weekend.

For more information about Camp Comfort, contact Sallie Wandling, director, who describes the camp as "God's Summer Home" for its incredible beauty, at 303-674-6400, or write to Mount Evans Hospice and Home Health Care, Inc., 3721 Evergreen Parkway, P.O. Box 2770, Evergreen, Colorado 80439.

EDUCATING AND INSPIRING THE WORLD

Brian Heinrich always felt uncomfortable with the conventional wisdom that all hemophiliacs are fragile. Today, after years of being physically active at camp, twenty-three-year-old Brian is working to dispel the fragility myth and to encourage hemophiliacs worldwide to experience the joy of physical activity in the beauty of the great outdoors.

As a child with hemophilia, I learned early on that when I got hurt, I simply didn't heal. People who do not have hemophilia normally produce a clotting factor in their blood to help them heal when they get cut or bruised. But, like all hemophiliacs, my body simply does not produce that clotting factor. Instead, when I pull a muscle, twist a joint, or cut myself, I need to intravenously administer a manufactured blood product to stop the bleeding.

When I was very young, I remember going for days hiding from my parents the fact that I was hurting until I just couldn't take the pain any longer. It wasn't that I liked to be in pain, it was that I hated equally to get shots. A needle in the vein was the only means to stop the pain and begin healing.

No matter how much I wanted to avoid going through that, I would end up waking up in the middle of the night in extraordinary pain, crying out to my parents. The process was exhausting. They would sometimes have to hold me down — or even tie me down — to stick me with a needle. It sounds terrible, but it was the only way.

I will never forget how my medicine at that time was this yellow fluid that looked just like urine. And it had to be kept frozen, so it was very cold when it went through my body. I knew my parents loved me.

And I knew they were doing all they could do to stop my pain. But at times, they just weren't able to find my tiny veins. Sometimes they had to poke me eleven or twelve times before they would finally get it in. The whole ordeal was excruciating.

My parents encouraged me to stay clear of most sporting activities to avoid serious injuries. They did not, however, want to see me going through life feeling physically limited. So at age seven, they started sending me to a camp for hemophiliacs at the Easter Seals Rocky Mountain Village in Colorado. I went to hemophilia camp for ten years, and I loved it every summer. I met so many kids from all over the United States, and I made so many great friends who also had hemophilia. Summers never came soon enough.

At camp, there was no need for a big discussion when a kid had a bleed. It was like open air — no big deal. And I really liked that. It was a nice, relaxing change from school, where you were always different and always having to explain things to people. One time at camp, we were fishing down at the lake when one kid got a hook stuck in him. That's what happens when kids are playing around with fishing lures and lines. So he had to go get treated. But that seemed normal to us, and the rest of us just went on fishing. At school, though, if something like that happened, it would have been cause for a big conversation and explanation. It was nice not having to explain to your friends that you were not going to bleed to death.

At hemophilia camp, I was introduced to all the physical activities that have become so much a part of my life and my world. That's where I learned to do what normal people do — but in an environment with other hemophiliacs around. I learned to rock climb. I learned to hike. I learned to ride horses — one of my favorites.

Even at camp, where I felt so free, the frustration of hemophilia was never far away. Sometimes I would be on a great hike, and totally loving it, and I would suddenly get a bleed. At other times, I wanted to start a certain activity, but I couldn't because I had a bleed right then. For me, and for the other campers, that was normal life. Our hemophilia was always a part of everything we did.

Camp taught me that I didn't have to live in fear. I could get involved in life. I could be a part of it. I learned that everyone has limitations, whether they are mental or physical, but those limitations don't have to stop you from living actively. I learned I had the ability to enjoy being physically active. And I learned I could encourage others to connect with those abilities inside themselves, too.

The doctors and nurses at camp also helped me discover this side of myself. They always encouraged us to go that extra mile. And if you did end up hurting yourself, then you learned how to deal with that, whether psychologically or physically. Every summer, I learned so much about my body. I realize now that that was one of the most important reasons we were there — to understand our bodies better — even though we thought we were there to be outdoors; to swim, ride horses, and shoot arrows.

My artistic abilities — another really important part of my life now — also started at camp. The camp's art room was a place of exploration, a place where you could do anything you wanted with Popsicle sticks and finger paints. Today, I use a computer to work with photographs. The work I do now is generally more technical than it was at camp. But working with watercolors today, I can still recall the freedom of expression I had when I was creating in that art room.

We also learned some things at camp that were unique to us as hemophiliacs. For example, many of us learned to self-transfuse. Self-transfusion was a big step in taking our health in our own hands. We no longer needed to rely on our parents to "stop the pain." We would be in the arts and crafts room and we would take a paper plate and turn it upside down and put gauze on one side and a piece of tourniquet hose on the other side. We'd fill the hose with water and practice sticking a needle through the gauze and plate into the hose. The gauze was supposed to be like skin, and the piece of hose was supposed to represent a vein. I will always remember this "art project" because the tube is huge and, in reality, your vein is so small! But it was clever, and we did learn from it.

Learning to transfuse at camp was very important because, for me, transfusing is a very intimate experience. The idea of sharing that with another person made me feel very vulnerable and open. I remember when I was fifteen, my best friend Christy wanted to help me transfuse one time. It felt really intimate to have her be a part of that, because that was just something I had always done by myself. So it was wonderful as a kid at camp to be able to talk about transfusing and see other kids doing it. In fact, without really realizing it, I looked forward to those times because it was such a special kind of connection with people.

This coming summer, my friend Lee, also a hemophiliac, and I are going to live out our dream of learning how hemophiliacs from other countries deal with their disease. We are starting at the World Confederation of Hemophilia meeting in Canada and are hoping to meet people we can stay with in Europe. We plan to backpack through Europe and Japan. Although we have contacts in Japan, we've heard that the Japanese don't like to talk about the disease much.

I'm going to take photographs on our trip and we plan to write a book. We want others to learn through our experiences. And we want them to be inspired to create their own experiences by talking about their disease and by trying new physical feats. We want to send a message that hemophilia does not have to limit their lives.

Hemophilia camp was the incredible beginning of this entire adventure — the adventure of building collective, intercontinental strength and inspiration for people with hemophilia.

— Brian Heinrich

Regarded as one of the top Easter Seals camps in the country, Rocky Mountain Village is fully accessible and used by more than 500 children and adults with disabilities for summer camp sessions. At Rocky Mountain Village, campers enjoy horseback riding, fishing, arts and crafts, dances, outdoor camping, hiking, and other camp activities.

For more information, write Rocky Mountain Village, Easter Seals Colorado Camp, P.O. Box 115, Empire, Colorado 80438; call 800-692-5520 or 303-569-2333, extension 301; or visit www.eastersealsco.org.

AN ELEVATED VIEW
OF THE WORLD

*Fourteen-year-old Rozalind Makowski, who has cerebral palsy, is the only
person in her small school who uses a wheelchair. Everyone knows her by name
and disability, but few people really know her. Roz knows that sometimes people
get scared and are at a loss for what to say or do when they're around her.
And she wishes those relationships were different. But when Roz goes riding,
she doesn't think about any of that. When she is helped onto the horse's back
and takes the reins in her hands, she and the horse are both ready to go.
She is then ready to ride trails she'd never be able to manage in a wheelchair,
and she can see the world from a whole new perspective.*

I was born with cerebral palsy. The part of my brain that signals my
muscles to work doesn't really work well. I have been through a lot of
surgeries and a lot of wheelchairs in my fourteen years.

My schoolmates tease me about being in a wheelchair. They yell,
"Roadblock. There's a roadblock in the hall," when they see me coming
down the hall in my power wheelchair. At first, I thought it was funny.
By now, though, it sounds kind of old and dumb to me.

On the other hand, some kids think it's one big picnic to have a
power wheelchair. They want to ride it. They want to drive it. But when
they act like it's so much fun, I know they don't have any idea what I've
been through. They don't understand the painful surgeries and the
painful therapy. They just think the wheelchair is cool.

To help me out, I have an aide with me pretty much everywhere I go.
She takes notes for me in class. One kid in the eighth grade tried to
hassle me and asked, "Why can't you write for yourself?" He knows I can

write, but I had to explain to him that it takes me a long time to write one paragraph. I do a lot on the computer, but that can take me a long time, too.

Two summers ago my therapist, who really understands me, recommended that I go to a therapeutic horseback riding program at Sheep Mountain Ranch in the Rocky Mountains. They asked me if I would like to ride a horse one day a week through the summer. I thought about how horses are gentle creatures and that I could pet them. And that made me think I could probably ride them, too.

So in June before sixth grade my dad loaded me into the car, and we drove to the ranch, which was right there in the mountains.

At the ranch, they told me I was going to ride an Appaloosa horse named "Sioux App," as in Sioux Indian Appaloosa. I was in awe when I saw that horse. He looked tall and sturdy and beautiful. But he looked gentle to me, too.

Four people helped me get out of my wheelchair and onto the horse. They carefully helped put one leg on each side of the saddle. At first, that part really hurt because my hips and legs were not used to being stretched like that.

I lowered myself into the soft saddle padded with rugs. Once I was settled in, I looked around and I was amazed. For the first time in my life, I was tall! I was on top of the world. My whole world fell into place when I sat on that saddle.

Since I'm always in a wheelchair, I'm always on a lower level than everyone else. And I spend so much time physically looking up at people. But when I was on Sioux App, people were looking up at me! It was an awesome feeling.

When Sioux App moved, I rocked in the saddle and that startled me. I shouted "Whoa!" But then I realized I wasn't going to fall off. And I laughed. I was on top of the world. For the first time ever, I had legs — four legs to move me.

It rained during my first ride — a soft rain. I rode for forty minutes and I wasn't tired a bit. I thought, "This is so much fun. I can really do this." When they helped me get off the horse that first time, my hips really hurt from being stretched. But that didn't even matter to me.

I knew I wanted to ride again and again.

I've been riding at the ranch now for two summers. We do so many things there. Sometimes I lead the horse through a bunch of logs on the ground or over a bundle of sticks. Sometimes I go out on a trail. Rose, the program director, puts little trinkets — like beads or handkerchiefs — on the trees for us to find. I love taking the horse on the trail.

Horses take me to places I would never get to go otherwise. And in the summer, it's beautiful to be on top of a horse while he is walking. I love to look up and look through the trees. It is so relaxing and peaceful.

When I am sitting on this animal and he is walking, it feels like I am walking. That is so cool for me. When I get off the horse, my legs feel like jelly. But that's a good feeling. So often my legs feel cramped or hurt from long hours of sitting in a wheelchair and not using them. But when I am on horseback, every part of my body feels better. Something in my body may hurt a little, but it's a good hurt.

And when the ride is done I brush the horse. I tie him up and I get to feed him a treat. We feed them. I hold the dish out for him to eat out of. He's got huge teeth and when he eats, it is like he is smiling. He doesn't seem to care that I am in a wheelchair.

I feel confident when I am on a horse. And when I'm finished riding, I feel a sense of accomplishment. I try to remember that great feeling when I have to do something that's hard for me. I think about how I controlled this large animal, led him, and trusted him with my body. I made sure that the horse didn't throw me off. I have never been thrown off, but I have almost fallen off. That's scary, but I take that risk because it's worth it to me.

I am the only wheelchair-bound person in my school. Sometimes I would feel like an outcast. I didn't want to have cerebral palsy. And I didn't deserve it. But God said I could deal with it. I don't want people to just see the chair. I want people to see past the chair. And that's what the helpers at the horseback-riding place do. They see me. And they see someone very capable of controlling a large animal. Horses don't judge me either. They just help me, help me to leave my wheelchair behind.

— *Rozalind Makowski*

SMaRT, a therapeutic horseback riding program, is located at the Sheep Mountain Ranch Therapeutic Riding Center in the Rocky Mountains. Several acres of pasture and space was provided by the YMCA for the riding arena. The group is affiliated with the North American Riding for the Handicapped Association, Inc. Most recently, SMaRT became part of the National Sports Center for the Disabled. NSCD provides a variety of therapeutic recreational services to individuals with special needs.

For more information about the SMaRT program write NSCD, P.O. Box 1290 Winter Park, Colorado 80482; call 970-726-1540; or visit www.nscd.org.

A PARENT'S PERSPECTIVE—
ADVENTUROUS RECOVERY

In April 1998 Hannah Gann was a healthy nine-year-old girl enjoying a
normal day at school. Then during gym class, she told the teacher she felt dizzy.
As she spoke the words, she fainted. Her face hit the hard gym floor.
Her front teeth pushed through her bottom lip. The teacher immediately called
the school nurse. As the teacher and other students focused on Hannah's
bleeding face, the nurse noticed Hannah was freezing up on her right side.
Instantly, she knew that Hannah was having a stroke. In that single moment,
Hannah's life — and the lives of her family — changed dramatically.
The difficulties and setbacks they have faced since then would have been hard
for them to imagine. But for one week that year, Queen Hannah braved the cold
and climbed high in the trees, both learning and teaching that
progress was an undeniable part of her future.

I was sitting in a staff meeting at work and noticed that my phone kept ringing nonstop. I had a feeling something was very wrong. And that's when the overhead page came indicating that I had an emergency phone call. It was the secretary at my daughter's school. She told me Hannah was going in and out of consciousness, and was being transported by ambulance to the hospital. She didn't say anything beyond that. Fear shot through my body. My mind was racing with questions. What could have happened? I was crying before I even hung up the phone. A co-worker grabbed her keys and told me she was taking me to the hospital.

When I first saw Hannah in the emergency room, I gasped at the sight of my daughter. It looked like she had been beaten up. She had two black eyes, a black swollen nose, and she was bleeding on the forehead and the chin. It was painful for me to look at her.

There was a great deal of confusion, with doctors speaking in medical terms to one another. I couldn't understand why they weren't fixing her nose and chin. When I spoke up and asked the doctor why weren't they fixing her face, he calmly said that that was not life-threatening and could wait.

"Life-threatening?"

Those words rung in my head. Before that moment, I hadn't wanted to believe the situation was that serious. I wanted to hang onto the thought that my daughter had just fallen.

After the doctors did the CAT scan and an MRI, they pulled my husband and me into a room and showed us the images. Even when they told us she had had a stroke, we were puzzled. We had never been around anyone who had had a stroke, so we didn't really grasp what it meant. They told us they were going to do a procedure to break up the three blood clots in her brain. But they couldn't tell us what the outcome would be.

The medical staff called in a stroke specialist from University of Colorado Hospital to do the procedure, which involved dripping medication directly on her brain. Hannah was only the second child in Colorado to have this procedure. After two and a half hours, the specialist told us it looked hopeful. Later, they told me she was a miracle child to have lived through it.

That first night was critical. Hannah drifted in and out of consciousness. She couldn't speak. Her right side was still frozen, and she was hooked up to quite a bit of machinery. All the doctors would say was that "time would tell." She was in the critical care unit for four days.

Hannah ended up staying in the hospital for thirty-two days. It was a big day when she was moved to a regular children's room on the rehabilitation floor. From there, she started speech, physical, and occupational therapy. Eventually, she began to show feeling on her right side.

Five days after she suffered the stroke, a clown came in and painted Hannah's face. When he finished, he smiled and asked if she wanted to see herself in the mirror. My husband and I held our breath. This was the first time Hannah would see herself in a mirror since the stroke. Even through the colorful clown make up, she was startled at the reflection. Until that moment, she hadn't realized how bad she looked. The right side of her face was drooping. Luckily, though, Hannah's face was the first part of her body to regain movement, and her lovely grin was back in place after two weeks of therapy.

Hannah's therapy involved many different types of activities and games. For example, she would stand balanced between two parallel bars and her therapist would set vinyl squeaky toys on the floor in front of her, encouraging Hannah to "squish that bug." And Hannah would step as hard as she could to make that bug squeak. She spent hours and hours in therapy, working her way up to seven or eight hours of therapy a day, five days a week.

Hannah came home in mid-May and continued her physical, speech, and occupational therapies. One day, the therapists told me about a camp the hospital sponsored for children with head injuries. They agreed Hannah had gained enough strength and independence over the past few months to take advantage of this type of therapy option.

I appreciated the information. But when the therapists said "head injury," I was taken off guard. I didn't make the connection between head injury and her stroke. It just sounded so strange to me.

Camp was at the end of July, about three months after her stroke. Hannah's summer was filled with tutoring and therapy, so she was really looking forward to going to camp. You could see the excitement on her face. Even though the hospital staff really worked to make her therapy fun, she like the idea of trading the gray and white hospital walls for a world filled with wildflowers, streams, and mountains.

The whole family went on the ride to take Hannah to camp. She was a celebrity because she was the only girl. Here was my little Hannah with all these little boys. But Hannah pointed out that there was one boy counselor and the rest of the counselors were girls, so it was kind of fair. Because she was the only girl, Hannah got a big, beautiful room with a private bathroom. She felt like a queen!

When it was time for us to go, Hannah didn't have any problem waving good-bye to her father and me. She was excited about her adventure for the next seven days. But leaving was difficult for us. And when we drove away, we realized it was the first time she had been away from us since the stroke.

Midweek, I got a call from the camp counselors. They told us, "Mom and Dad, she is doing just great, and she doesn't miss you at all." It's kind of funny, but we were overjoyed to hear that.

The counselor told me that one night the group had planned to do some tent camping. Since it was cold, though, most of the kids had wanted to go back and sleep in the cabins. But not Hannah. Hannah was the only one to stay outside the whole night. It was really cold, but she went right to sleep. One counselor stayed out there with her, but he didn't get any sleep because he was so cold. In the morning, when Hannah didn't see any of the others outside with her, she thought she had overslept. She was so surprised to hear she was the only kid to sleep outside all night. That made her feel brave! She braved the cold.

When we picked Hannah up after seven days, she told us all about her activities: rock climbing, canoeing, swimming, climbing the ropes course. Camp had really broken the monotony of her therapy. And she had never seen her camp activities as therapy. They were just adventures to her.

Camp brought out an unshakable determination in Hannah. It built up her physical strength as well as her confidence. When she got home, she was ready to go out and get the world.

Hannah continues to work hard at the physical rehabilitation. Now, schoolwork is the more challenging aspect of recovery. With strokes, it takes generally a year for the victim to regain endurance. Brain injuries take a very long time to heal, so the schoolwork and mental exercise are very tiring for Hannah. But whenever she finds herself in a taxing situation, Hannah just taps into the determination she experienced at camp. And it gets her through.

— Sherry Gann

The Children's Hospital of Denver provides a camp option through Camp Zenith for children 8–18 years old who have traumatic brain injuries. Professionals from the rehabilitation department work with wilderness educators at the Breckenridge Outdoor Education Center to plan activities involving hiking, rock climbing, canoeing, overnight camping, a ropes course, and arts and crafts.

For more information, write to The Children's Hospital Handicapped Sports Program, 1056 E. 19th Avenue, P.O. Box 385, Denver, Colorado 80218; call 303-861-6590; or visit www.tchden.org.

Photograph © John Fielder 2001

HOLDING THE REINS
OF A DREAM

*Four years ago, Adam Brooks was a twelve-year-old who was struggling in
school because of a learning disability. Then he discovered his passion for horses.
Today, two years before high school graduation, he is busy researching colleges
to find the school with the best equestrian program. He knows he holds the
reins to his future. Adam is committed to becoming an expert rider —
and he has his sights set on the Olympics. But he also understands that doing
well in school, no matter how difficult, is part of that path.*

I have always had a hard time in school. It's a struggle for me to get
decent grades. My parents didn't always understand why I wasn't catch-
ing on, and sometimes my mom would yell at me to get me to try harder.
All of us — my parents, my teachers, and I — were frustrated.

I had a lot of trouble with reading. It seemed like the material just
wasn't clicking with me. Days at school seemed really long. I just looked
forward to a time when I would never have to go to school again.

One of the teachers suggested to my mom that I get tested for a
learning disability. At first my mom didn't understand what the teacher
meant. When she heard the word "disability" she thought they were
talking about something being physically wrong, something she should
be able to see. But they tested me, and we all found out I did have a
learning disability.

Even with knowing that, school is still a struggle. But today I have
motivation to do well. I have found something that makes everything
worthwhile. Horses.

When I was five years old, my uncle took me on a trail ride in
Arizona. The memory of that ride had never left me. My mom would take
me to the toy store and I would dart to where I could find the collection

of toy horses. I started using my allowance to buy toy horses, and pretty soon my room was filled with them.

When I was twelve years old, my mom found out about a program in the city called the Urban Farm. She signed me up for the program. It cost $20 to ride once a week for nine weeks. I was so happy. I hadn't been on a horse since that first ride with my uncle.

I started on Sequoia, the biggest horse at the Farm. Right away, I felt like I had a connection with her. After that first ride, Sequoia would come right to me when she heard my voice or saw me. I would call her name, and she would run to the fence. She had never done that for anyone else. She would follow me in the yard, like a family dog follows its owner. I didn't have to put a bridle or a rope on her. It was kind of amazing. I sort of spoiled her with lots of love and treats. I brought her carrots. She was like my kid — a big, two-ton kid.

A long time ago, before she was donated to the Farm, Sequoia got her head caught in an electric fence. Because of that, she shook her head a lot, and sometimes acted like she was crazy, but I stuck with her. Angel, one of the ladies who worked and taught riding at the Farm, told me no one else could control Sequoia. Angel said I had a gentle hand, and the horse respected me. I felt good about that because I thought Sequoia was a pretty horse.

Eventually I became good enough to begin competitive riding. Unfortunately, I had to switch horses then because Sequoia was not a competitive riding horse. Although I don't ride her anymore, she still comes to the fence to have me pet her. I still bring her carrots.

My second year, I began riding dressage on Dakota. Dressage is like dancing while on horseback. The rider needs to stay still, sit up tall, and guide the horse through a series of moves. It's a big sequence of steps to memorize. In school I would have trouble memorizing things. But with riding, I just kept riding until I got the pattern down in my head. I went to my first competition in dressage with Dakota.

In the middle of the night before the competition I woke up and ran through the pattern in my head. I didn't eat breakfast that morning because I was too nervous. I was anxious about the event on the way over in the car. Another rider from the Farm, Travis, who was ten years old, wanted to help me before the show. He polished my boots and made sure my number was pinned on straight. It made me feel like a rich person to have him doing all that stuff. I was afraid that I was going to forget everything. When I finally got on the horse, my mom says my shoulders squared back and I stretched my body up straight and high. She said

I looked really confident. It seemed like a lifetime in the ring to do that pattern in front of the judges, but I did it. Before I got on the horse I was terrified. After I finished, I was proud of myself for competing and doing well.

Two years ago, I started working at the Farm. It was my first job. I work two nights a week, feeding forty horses. It takes a lot of time and it's scary in the barn when it gets dark. But even though I get scared, I love being at the Farm. And I always show up to do my job.

Last year, Cindy LeFevre, an Olympic rider, came to the Farm. She watched me ride and asked me if I wanted to work on her farm for the summer in exchange for private lessons. She had some really expensive and beautiful thoroughbred horses. I would work eight hours a day mucking the stalls, loading hay, and feeding, and brushing the horses. Cindy made sure I was doing everything right, so I really learned a lot just working there. The lesson she gave me was always hard, always a real challenge. But she believes I can be a great rider. I feel really good about that.

Being around horses is something I really like. I love the strength of the horses. I love their power and the fact that I can get on top of a horse and feel confident. I believe I can do anything on a horse.

If I am having a bad day at school — because school is still tough — I can come to the Farm and feel good again. I am relaxed around the horses. I do things I know I can do. And I know I can handle the responsibilities. Some days I don't want to go to school because it's hard — but I always want to come to the Farm. And, I have to do my homework before I ride. My mom won't let me come to the Farm, even to work, if my grades aren't okay. That motivates me.

Now that I am in the advanced riders group. I have a contract I had to sign with Angel. It has my riding goals. It says what I am going to do with dressage, and it lists my competition goals. Riding is a start, but there are other things in that contract I had to agree to. It has academic achievements I agree to meet. That can be tough, but it's worth it to ride. I also made a promise to Angel and my parents that I will stay drug, alcohol, and tobacco free.

When I graduate from high school in two years, I want to go to an equestrian college. This spring break, I want to go look at Colorado State University because that college has a great equestrian program. I am more focused now than I used to be. And I'm learning to plan farther ahead than just next week. My goal is to make the Olympic team in six to eight years. It's much more than a dream. It's something I am really working for.

When I was having trouble in school before coming to the Farm, I never thought I could be this good at something. This program — being able to ride — gives me a reason to do well in school. When my mom was pressuring me, that didn't work to motivate me. I just got frustrated trying to do better. Now, it's still hard, but it's all worth it.

I am dedicated to things now because this program has given me self-confidence. I have a wall full of ribbons and various trophies at home. It feels good to win those. It's the best feeling ever to know I did it and all the work paid off.

I have more than 130 horses — model horses of all kinds. Sometimes I line them up and put them on my bed. I show my mom a figurine and tell her which ones I am going to own.

Before this program, all I wanted was just to get through the grind of school. Now, riding gives me hope and dreams.

— *Adam Brooks*

The Urban Farm at Stapleton, Colorado, provides agricultural and environmental education to urban children, youth, and their families. Situated on 23 acres, the Farm is a place where young people and their families in the Denver area can experience Colorado's agrarian roots. Through those experiences, they can develop a sense of responsibility for the well-being of the environment and learn to live compatibly with others both — humans and animals.

For more information, write to The Urban Farm at Stapleton, 10200 Smith Road, Denver, Colorado 80239; call 303-307-9332; or visit www.theurbanfarm.org.

© Padgett McFeely 2001

WEARING CONFIDENCE

Most adults are sensitive to the needs and feelings of a child with an
obvious disability. But learning disabilities are often invisible —
and even when people are told about them, some don't believe they exist.
So it's easy for people who are ignorant or insensitive to hurt the feelings
of a child with a learning disability. Peter Archer knew all about those hurt
feelings by the time he was seven years old. He dealt with them every day.
But at camp, he finally found what he needed: acceptance and assistance.
And although he wore the same clothes all week, Peter dressed himself in a
new confidence his parents had never seen before.

I was diagnosed with attention deficit with hyperactivity disorder (ADHD) and dysfunctional sensory integration (DSI) when I was six years old. My teacher noticed that small noises or movements were mesmerizing to me. I would focus on the smallest of things until the next distraction caught my attention. In addition to that, the DSI made it slower for my system to process, organize, and understand information detected through my senses. So I was labeled a slow learner because it took me longer to process what was being said to me.

When I was invited to a friend's house, my parents would talk to those parents about my ADHD and the DSI. The other parents would smile and say it wasn't a problem. But it was a problem. And I would never be invited back to play.

Because of the DSI, my coordination wasn't always that good. For me, doing some of the simple gym and outdoor recess activities could be very intimidating. After a while, I got so discouraged, I just wouldn't even try. And the other kids would tease me.

Because of my learning disabilities, I didn't have a clue about the meaning of common social cues, even those passed among preschoolers. My classmates were frustrated because I couldn't understand what they were trying to tell to me. And I was frustrated and confused by their reactions to me.

Many days, I came home completely puzzled and in tears and said to my mom, "I don't understand it. My best friend hauled off and hit me because he wanted me to be quiet, but I didn't know he wanted me to be quiet."

In reality, my friend probably had thrown all kinds of social cues my way. He probably gave me a look, made a "shhhhh" sound, or nudged me in the ribs. But because I wasn't able to pick up on any of those signals, all of his efforts would go right past me, until he finally got my attention by slugging me. Then he'd shout, "Be quiet!" But it was news to me that I was even being loud.

During the summer, my mom tried to get me involved in organized sports. But it just didn't work for me because I had too many distractions. Instead of tuning into the sport, I "zoned out." So much was happening around me — kids laughing and shouting to each other, kids running and throwing balls, the coaches shouting instructions — that I couldn't understand as quickly as the other kids seemed to. Kids started teasing me because I wasn't where I was supposed to be. Coaches started talking to me like I wasn't very smart. To the coach I appeared uncooperative and to the other kids I was just a goof. On top of all of that, I was having trouble understanding directions, and I had trouble with my coordination.

My coordination difficulties put me at a real disadvantage. How was I supposed to hit a "little" ball with a bat when I couldn't even catch a "big" beachball? It felt awful to see how unskilled I was when I compared my skills to those of the other kids.

My parents tried sending me to a day camp, but I only lasted one day. It was a lamentable experience. It seemed like there were a million kids and only two counselors. It was sensory overload for me, and my brain was working overtime processing all the stimulation. It was as if my brain was a computer that was trying to run too many applications at once. My computer-brain crashed. It froze up. And no one had the time to help one little kid to "reboot." I cried. I felt completely unprepared for the day, as if I were in school and had forgotten all my homework.

Then my mom found out about Little Tree Camp, a camp for kids with ADHD and DSI, through The Children's Hospital.

The first time I went to Little Tree Camp I was seven years old. It was my first time away from Mom and Dad. I was so excited that I jumped out of the back seat of my parents' car when we got there. But I was quickly overwhelmed. My eyes saw what looked like an endlessly large, open area in the mountains. It was hard for me to comprehend all this space. This felt completely unstructured to me. I just stood there holding my suitcase. As kid with DSI, I was most comfortable with a lot of structure.

My life at home was full of structure and that was good for me. I knew that when my mom came into my room and sang our good-morning song, that meant it was time to get out of bed and begin the day. I learned to dress myself, but my choices for clothes for the day were very limited so that I would not become confused or overwhelmed by having to select from an entire closet full of clothes. My clothing never had any zippers, buttons, snaps, or laces because they were difficult and frustrating for me to use. Breakfast was always the same because it was reassuring not to be surprised. The rest of everyday life was surprising enough.

I knew that after breakfast my mom would drive me to school. During the trip we talked about what I would be doing at school that day and about the teachers and children I would be seeing that day. This planning and repetition helped me feel more relaxed. It helped me know what to expect that day.

My mom had known I might feel overwhelmed with camp being a new environment, so she had tried to create some structure for me through my suitcase. Inside the case she had neatly packed five complete outfits, each in its own plastic bag. Each bag was clearly labeled with a day of the week. And she put my toothbrush and toothpaste in a bag. She put in a bag labeled "extra underwear." She tried to help me feel comfortable.

The first year at camp I was so scared. My mind was racing with panic: How would I know it was time to wake up? What if breakfast wasn't what I expected? What if the other kids could do everything better and faster than me?

The counselors greeted me as soon as I got out of the car. They introduced themselves and told me they thought we would be good friends and that they wanted me to have the best time ever. They did not talk too fast, and they waited patiently for me to answer. They gave me simple choices that I could handle.

That first day we said good-bye to our parents and put our things in order at the campground. We had lots of help. The poor counselors were able to get about two hours of sleep that night because we all were afraid of sleeping in an unfamiliar place and we stayed awake almost the whole night. The other kids were just like me — different.

Our camp experience started with a climb up a sixty-foot-high ropes course. This was something the counselors all thought we were capable of doing. But successfully negotiating the course meant overcoming our fears and gaining confidence in ourselves and forgetting our past experiences of frustration and failure.

Wearing fitted harnesses, we began our climb over a suspension bridge that shakes and quivers as you walk over it. From the bridge you step onto a six-foot platform. A thick telephone pole is centered in the platform. As you progress on the course, the poles become thinner and the platforms become smaller. The smallest platform is about two feet by two feet. On the first level the platforms are about forty feet from the ground. With each new task, the platforms are placed higher and higher on the poles. The last platform is about sixty feet above the ground. Each new obstacle is more difficult than the last and requires more confidence and skill.

The fear I felt during the ropes course made my legs shake until it felt as if I were trying to walk with both of my feet asleep. I was afraid of heights; I would look down and shake. But all the counselors and the other campers shouted encouragement to me while I was on the course and praised me enthusiastically. I never had so much support. It didn't throw me off — it made me feel good. I was scared, but I was happy.

Other days at camp we celebrated water, earth, and nature. We went canoeing, rock climbing, and hiking.

The counselors definitely got more sleep after the first night. By the time we turned in for the evening, we were wiped out from a great day of activity and discovery. I think building confidence brings on a good exhaustion. The next day my parents were coming to get me. I couldn't wait to tell them all about my camp adventure.

Much to their horror, though, when my parents picked me up, I was wearing the same clothes I had worn when they dropped me off five days before! The clothes in the suitcase remained untouched. I had not changed once. The counselors urged me to change, but I was unsure about so many things, that I just didn't. The counselors decided that wasn't what was important that week, and they let me stay in my same clothes throughout the week.

I could have left with the same bag for camp the next year. Along with not changing my clothes I stopped brushing my teeth after the first

night. Holding a toothbrush requires fine-motor skills, a real challenge for me. At the time, my mind was swimming with all newness of the day. We were brushing our teeth on the porch the first night. I was not focused on brushing my teeth and was not even aware of what I was doing. And I dropped my toothbrush between the slats and we couldn't get it out. So I didn't brush my teeth the whole week either.

Despite staying in the same clothes all week and working up some wicked bad breath, I had the time of my life at camp. At the end I felt so good about myself. At age seven I had experienced the feeling of independence. I survived a whole week without my parents. I had figured things out on my own. I went on hikes with the group and I didn't get lost. I climbed a rock wall and rappelled down. The counselors showed us how to skip rocks. I had never done that before. I survived a tough ropes course.

I remember I was stuck on one part of the ropes course and another kid helped me figure it out. That was such a different response for me. Usually kids snapped at me when I didn't understand how to do something. But at camp other kids were helping me. I received an out-of-the-blue positive response. I wasn't used to that. It felt really good to me.

It was terrific to find out that other kids had similar learning disabilities. In the understanding and caring environment of Little Tree Camp we were all able to work together and we got along great. We were allowed the time we needed to figure things out on our own, and we were given assistance whenever it was necessary.

At the end of the first visit to camp, I was excited to see my parents. I talked nonstop. That was a 180-degree difference from when they would pick me up after school and I would be in tears. I jumped with excitement to show them our camp tepee, the ropes course, and to tell them about climbing. I introduced them to my new friends. To say they were stunned is somewhat of an understatement. Here I was, in the same clothes they dropped me off in. I smelled. But I was more excited about life than I had ever been. For the first time, my parents felt hopeful for me. They had never seen me filled with such joy.

My parents were afraid that I would have a difficult time at camp and not fit in, but they knew that it was something they couldn't help me with. And here I went to camp, made friends, and accomplished difficult physical activities — and I was genuinely happier than I had ever been in my life.

My mom says that's when she knew everything was going to be all right. To see me all smiles was a real thrill for my parents. I guess it was the first time they had felt joy like that, too.

When school started again in the fall I was a celebrity. For the first time in my life, I had a story to share with other kids. I was able to brag about my accomplishments. They sat and listened to my story. Not many seven-year-olds had climbed a rock wall or done a ropes course, so they were pretty interested in the details. They also were amazed that my parents weren't with me. It was such a boost for me. I was actually cocky about the whole thing for a little while — such a new attitude for me. It was great to have something to brag about.

For the first time in my life, I really believed I could do anything if I just set my mind to it. I learned that it was okay to slow down and think about what I wanted to do. I finally had the confidence that I needed to work toward long-term goals. That feeling just kept building each year as I went to camp. Each year at Little Tree Camp boosted my confidence. Each year I went farther on the ropes course, climbed higher on the climbing wall, and rowed faster in the canoe. Each year I learned more about myself and not just about my ADHD–DSI. I learned things I could do instead of being reminded of the things I couldn't do. I learned constructive ways of coping with and compensating for my learning differences. I was reassured that I was not alone and that being different could sometimes be an asset. Little Tree Camp reminded me each year that even when others thought I had nothing to offer and saw only my disabilities, I could value myself and my talents and I could be confident about myself.

I was a camper at Little Tree every summer for eight years. Then last year, at fifteen, I became a mentor. That year I met Brad. He was an eight-year-old boy who was really scared of heights. He would put one foot on the rock-climbing wall and then wouldn't move. He wouldn't put his foot down because he knew if he did he wouldn't go back up. But he was too scared to move the other foot off the floor to start up the wall. I talked to Brad until he felt safe and confident enough to start climbing up the wall.

I believe that when Brad climbed that wall, it changed his life. He was so excited. When my parents came to get me, Brad ran to them and announced he was my best friend. Brad told them what a good time he had with me. It was great to share Brad's victory.

Camp affected my parents' lives as well as mine. It boosted their confidence in my future. They said they saw the gifts in me. My mom says the world suffers because many people assume some things are impossible. But I look at the world differently and see different possibilities. She says that's my gift. I think my positive experience at camp that first year helped me realize that I might have a gift.

It's okay to be unique.

— *Peter Archer*

The Children's Hospital of Denver provides a camp option for children eight to twelve years old with sensory integration dysfunction, learning delays, and attention deficits through its Little Tree Camp. Occupational therapists collaborate with wilderness educators from the Breckenridge Outdoor Education Center to plan activities including rock climbing, canoeing, a ropes course, journaling, and craft projects. Focus is placed on developing independence, competence, social skills, and self-confidence.

For more information, write to The Children's Hospital Handicapped Sports Program, Little Tree Camp, 1056 E. 19th Avenue, P.O. Box 385, Denver, Colorado 80218, or call 303-861-6590. For more information on DSI, visit www.sinetwork.org.

NO LONGER ALONE

Long before he was diagnosed, Justin E. understood the concept of epilepsy.
He had cared for his miniature Dachshund, Snickers, through many seizures.
He took responsibility to ensure that Snickers ate her medication to help keep
the seizures at bay. Then at age eleven, Justin learned that he, too, had epilepsy.
Understanding the concept of epilepsy and actually having the disorder were
two different and very scary things. Yet he chose to keep his epilepsy a secret.
Only his parents, sister, and doctors knew the challenges he wrestled with, and
how alone he sometimes felt. But all that changed one weekend when he had the
chance to mix an outdoor adventure with discussions about epilepsy.

Last year, I agreed to talk to a group of representatives from a drug company about the medications I was taking for my epilepsy. The drug reps asked me about what life was like when I started showing signs that I had epilepsy. I was blank. I didn't have an answer. Although I was diagnosed with epilepsy two years earlier — when I was eleven years old and in the fifth grade — it was at that instant that my mom and I both realized that I had little memory of the early stages of the disease. So my mom jumped in to answer their questions.

It had all started with my mom finding me one morning in a wet bed. That was unusual for a kid my age, but even more unusual for me because I hadn't wet the bed much even as a little boy. And until she pointed it out, I hadn't known anything had happened.

Another time, I went to the grocery store with my parents. My dad started to ask me a question about something. But when he turned to look at me, he saw that the front of my pants were soaked. I didn't even know I had wet my pants.

Neither my parents nor I had any idea about what was going on. My pediatrician ran tests that checked for a bladder problem. According to the tests, everything was okay. But the problem kept getting worse.

I would be sitting in class and the next thing I knew, my pants would be wet. I don't remember it too much, but I know the kids in school made fun of me.

My mom said while they were still trying to figure out where the problem was, I started acting like a child. I would bring my stuffed animals to the table with me, and tell my mom, "I am five today," or "I am six today." Then I would act that age.

That's when my parents realized this was not just a bladder problem, and my mom really started to panic. She called the pediatrician and said they had to figure out what was going on soon or I would suffer long-term emotional problems. As an elementary school teacher, she knew that there was only so much emotional trauma that a child could take before he would develop damaging emotional scars. My dad thought it might be epilepsy. My parents also thought it could be a brain tumor.

While the doctors were wondering what to do, my parents tried a test on me at home. While I was sitting on the couch and they were talking to me, my dad threw some nonsense words into his sentence. I knew my dad had said something strange, but I couldn't say anything for a moment.

My parents told the doctor about their test, and he asked me if I remembered anything about that moment. When I thought about it, I realized I had had a tingly feeling in my brain, in my head somewhere, right then. It wasn't as tingly as when your foot falls asleep, but it was back there. That was the first time I put some words to what was going on.

The doctor ordered an EEG to see how the nerves in my brain were working, and he called my parents immediately with the test results. The test showed that I was having seizures, and that I was actually unconscious one or two seconds out of every ten. This would happen throughout the whole day. The doctor said my parents might not see the seizures, but my teachers would probably see the difference in my learning.

Next, they had to do an MRI test to find out why I was having all the seizures. I had to lie perfectly still in a big tube while x-ray machines took pictures of my brain. It was very noisy and scary. Before the test my dad gave me a Beanie Baby monkey to hold so I wouldn't be so scared. The MRI showed that my brain looked normal; no tumors. Then they knew it was epilepsy.

Pretty soon, my seizures started lasting eight to ten seconds, and sometimes I would unconsciously walk around while I had them. One

morning I was up brushing my teeth in the upstairs bathroom, and ended up standing in the living room holding my toothbrush. I didn't know what I was doing there or how I got there.

My parents have said it was like traveling to eternity and back to find the right medication for me. It took nearly six months. Some medications just didn't work for me. One medication changed my personality and made me aggressive. That's when my parents told the doctors to try a different medication because they didn't want to lose the personality of the boy they knew and loved.

Finally, we found a medication that worked, and life seemed pretty normal except for the side effects: trembling and slowness in thought processing. That wasn't a big deal in the summer. But when I went back to school in the fall, school became really difficult. Math became very hard for me. Memorizing facts was impossible. The medicine made my hands shake, so it was hard to write quickly — or in cursive. That's a lot to have going on when a teacher is speaking and you are trying to take notes.

School became kind of a struggle. I had to work really hard at home every night just to keep my grades up. But I never gave up.

Some days, I came home from school feeling down. I told my mom I felt different from everyone else. She told me I was just like other kids. I looked like other kids. I talked like other kids. But I would say, "They don't take medicine like I do."

I kept my epilepsy a secret. The only people who knew about my epilepsy were my doctors and my family. I never told any of my friends. I was pretty private and confidential about the whole thing. But my parents knew I needed to talk. I kept it all a secret because some people may not understand what epilepsy is and being different from everybody is hard. Instead of trying to tell them, I just decided not even to tell them about it. I only told people who had to know because it was just over-whelming emotionally. My parents did tell adults, like teachers, who needed to know and always asked them to respect my privacy.

My parents found out about a camp for children with epilepsy through The Children's Hospital. My first reaction when I heard about camp was that I wanted to go. I was worried about being away from my parents — I had stuck pretty close to them since my diagnosis — but I decided to go anyway.

My parents drove me to the hospital where I met all the other kids who were going that summer. The nurses and camp counselors piled us into vans and took us to camp. I remember that we played a superhero game to help us learn each other's names. I was Justin the Justice Maker.

There were about ten kids on the trip, and all of us had epilepsy. At camp, we explored and found dinosaur tracks. We swam in the Colorado River. We listened to scary stories by a campfire. And we learned about what epilepsy meant in the lives of other kids.

During my first summer at camp, I was in an outrigger canoe with another boy when he had a convulsive seizure. The counselor who was with us tried to hold him so he wouldn't fall out, and I held onto the sides. It was one of the first times I ever saw a kid having a seizure like that. I felt comfortable because I was not the only one who had seizures.

We'd eat pizza or spaghetti at dinner and we would talk about sports, school, mods, and epilepsy. One girl talked about how she felt just before a seizure, and that made me think about my own feelings right before a seizure. One boy told us that he always ate pudding with his medication. And one of the counselors told us he had had epilepsy as a small child. I learned a lot about epilepsy that first summer. But mostly, I learned I wasn't alone.

Before camp ended, I exchanged e-mail addresses with the other kids. It helped me a lot to know there were others out there who could understand how I felt sometimes. And after camp, I didn't feel so isolated any more. My mom says I didn't come home all bubbly and ready to tell the world about my disease, but she knew I felt more at ease about having epilepsy. She said I had this new kind of calmness in knowing that I wasn't the only one who had to struggle with it.

If I hadn't had the camp experience, I don't know when I ever would have met other kids with epilepsy. The Epilepsy Foundation now has a teen chat room, so I visit that. But at camp I got to go hiking and canoeing with other kids like me and talk face to face with them about epilepsy. Just like my mom says, kids understand other kids. Nobody but a kid can know what it is like to walk into middle school with epilepsy.

— *Justin E.*

The Children's Hospital of Denver provides a camp option for children eight to eighteen years old who have epilepsy through its Epilepsy Wilderness Camp Program. Professionals from the rehabilitation department work with wilderness educators at the Breckenridge Outdoor Education Center to plan activities involving hiking, rock climbing, canoeing, overnight camping, a ropes course, and arts and crafts.

For more information, write to The Children's Hospital, 1056 E. 19th Avenue, Denver, Colorado 80218; or call 303-864-5827.

Photograph © John Fielder 2001

FREEDOM FOUND ON ONE SKI

*Born with one leg, Allison Jones has never shied away from trying
everything life has to offer. At age five, she strapped on one ski and glided down
the bunny hill. Within three years, she had outgrown simple downhill skiing.
Her desire for speed took her to the top of higher, longer runs. This desire,
along with unwavering fortitude, also took her to the top in competitive skiing.
Today, at age fifteen, Allison is the National Disabled Junior Champion
in skiing and is well on her way to competing in the disabled Olympics.
To Allison, there is nothing more inspiring and inviting than the untouched
white canvas of snow on a mountain.*

I was born with a birth defect called proximal femoral focal deficiency, which means I was born without a thigh. The lower part of my leg was attached directly to my pelvis by skin and muscles at birth. I was born with a full foot, but when I was nine months old, my mom had to make the hard decision to have it surgically removed so I could wear a prosthesis. From the very beginning, my mom didn't want me thinking I was any different from any other kid just because I had a deformity. So she taught me to be tough in the face of teasing.

The teasing started as soon as I entered school. Here I was in kindergarten and I was getting into fistfights with other kids. My mom had always told me to ignore the teasing. But sometimes it got to be too much and I would fight. It was like that all through school. When I was in the sixth grade, I was suspended three times for fighting.

But when I was skiing, all those troubles left my mind.

When I was five, my mom, who is active in a lot of sports, wanted to find a family sport that she and my younger sister, Haley, and I could all do together. I loved swimming, but Haley didn't. Haley loved hiking, but

I was terrible at walking. My mom thought skiing might be the answer. So she took us to Winter Park, a ski resort in Colorado, strapped a ski on my good leg and gave me a little push. I glided down this small incline, balancing on one ski.

I liked it right away.

Walking can be painful for me because putting pressure on the prosthesis can make my stump ache. But this was like floating. When I walked, I felt like I had to drag my leg through water. But with skiing there was no pounding or forcing it to move. I could let it just hang — but I was in motion.

Since Haley and I both liked skiing, the three of us went back a couple more times that year. The next year, when I was six, the National Sports Center for the Disabled sponsored me with a free ski, lessons, and lift pass for the season. I skied every weekend I could when I was six and seven.

At age eight, my instructor told me he had nothing more to teach me. By that time, I was skiing down the hill really well by myself. So he sent me to the competition center to check out the disabled racing program.

That same afternoon, I tried skiing the racecourse. I borrowed a pair of outriggers, which are like crutches that have ski tips at the bottom. The outriggers helped me balance through the turns. I didn't have a clue about the technically correct way to ski a racecourse. I was just flying through the gates as fast as I could. It was so exciting.

From then on, every weekend, I would work on skiing faster through the gates. Before too long, I became fast enough to compete. So at age eight, I was the youngest person on the disabled team. Disabled racing, at that time, was divided by disability, not age. Everyone else was at least twenty. I didn't have the weight behind me to ski against the adults, but every time I pushed off from that starting gate, I was skiing as hard as I could. And I have been racing ever since.

I am driven to be a great racer. Skiing is freedom to me. A lot of time my body hurts, whether it's my back, my stump, or my hips. But when I am skiing, I forget about the pain. My thoughts are focused on getting through those gates in record time. Skiing is second nature to me. I put on skis and I feel right at home. I know I can do anything on skis.

It's not easy to get out of bed at 5:30 a.m. to go skiing. But it makes me happy when I am there first thing in the morning — it feels awesome to see the mountain covered in white. The atmosphere is wide open. In the early morning, the other disabled racers and I can ski the backside of the mountain, away from the tourists. We aren't stuck in anyone's rules about how fast we can go. I can create turns. I can do anything.

Photo courtesy of NSCD

It's awesome to make fresh tracks — to be the first one down the mountain. And then when I ride the chairlift back up after a first run, I can look down and see the ski tracks I have drawn in the snow.

— *Allison Jones*

The National Sports Center for the Disabled (NSCD) — which began in 1970 as a one-time ski lesson for 23 amputee children — has evolved into the largest and most successful program of its kind in the world. In addition to recreational downhill and cross-country skiing, snow-boarding, and snowshoeing lessons, NSCD provides year-round competition training for ski racers with disabilities.

For more information, write to the National Sports Center for the Disabled, P.O. Box 1290, Winter Park, Colorado 80482; call 970-726-1540 or 303-316-1540; or visit www.nscd.org.

AFTERWORD

Dori Biester, PhD, RN
President and CEO
The Children's Hospital
Denver, Colorado

Poets and philosophers have tried through the centuries to express just how nature and the outdoors restore the body, mind, and spirit. Innumerable works of art have as a starting point the inspiration of the sunrise, hills, and valleys and what they offer us in a reflective and healing way. Even recordings of the sound of running water and of the forest can soothe us. Henry David Thoreau said, "I went to the woods because I wished to live deliberately, to front only the essential facts of life, and see if I could not learn what it had to teach."

Introducing young people to nourishing experiences in the outdoors is something that benefits them in ways we might not completely fathom, but that we instinctively know to be important. The return to the simple — roasting a marshmallow, pitching a tent, contemplating a rushing stream — reminds us that we don't need much to live well after all. These things reconnect us with who we are in the most primary terms. I was touched by the joy that Nathan Brainard expressed in being able to make and eat his own peanut-butter-and-jelly sandwich! We should all be so richly sensitized to the little pleasures in life.

Some young people struggling with illness or injury spend their days concentrating on what's not working in their lives. In these natural environments, they can focus positively on just being *kids* — on making friends and having fun.

As caregivers, we too are helped and healed by these young spirits. As one therapist wrote, "The magic at camp occurs when these kids invite the child in us to participate in pirate adventures, kazoo parades, and bear hunts. Observing such honesty, lack of inhibition, and determination helps us to see portions of life through a child's eyes. When we can meet on common ground without preconceived ideas of what should or should not be possible, the potential is endless."

I believe these stories will stir and challenge you. I hope also that you will return to this book as a source of strength and inspiration.

— *Dori Biester, PhD, RN*